COYOTE'S SONG

COLLECTED POEMS AND SELECTED ART

CARLOS CORTÉZ KOYOKUIKATL

Edited by Carlos Cumpián
and David Ranney

With commentary by
René Arceo, Carlos
Cumpián and Fred Sasaki

• Chicago •

Grateful acknowledgement to the National Museum of Mexican Art for permission to use permanent collection images from the Carlos Cortéz' files and to include the poetry and images originally published in Cortéz' book *de Kansas a Califas & Back to Chicago* (1992) and from Carlos Cumpián's *Coyote Sun* (1990) both published by MARCH Abrazo Press.

Design and Typesetting: Taylor Sanderson
Carlos Cortéz Portrait: Hector Duarte, portrait photographer: Juan L. Cruz
Carlos Cortéz cartoon panel: Jay Lynch
Carlos Cortéz original color photo (1988): Carlos Cumpián
Carlos Cortéz' Scratchboard, Linocuts and Block Prints:
National Museum of Mexican Art, MARCH Abrazo Press

Library of Congress Cataloging-in-Publication Data

Names: Cortéz, Carlos, 1923-2005, author. | Cumpián, Carlos, editor, writer of added commentary. | Ranney, David C., editor. | Sasaki, Fred, writer of added commentary. | Arceo-Frutos, René H., writer of added commentary.
Title: Coyote's Song : Collected Poetry and Selected Art / Carlos Cortéz ; edited by Carlos Cumpián and David Ranney ; with commentary by René Arceo, Carlos Cumpián and Fred Sasaki
Description: Chicago, IL : MARCH Abrazo Press, 2023. | Includes bibliographical references.|
Summary: "Carlos Cortéz, Koyokuikatl (1923-2005) has left a magnificent legacy of political poetry along with visual images using scratchboard, linocut and block prints. But he also left us the example, captured in this book, of tireless activism, including his poetry and art, all directed toward a new society. That lifetime venture, in his words, was to contribute to "a society that is more egalitarian, more loving of each other, more recognizing of the worth in each of us." This book contains his poems, visual art, and commentaries on his life's work by some of those closest to him" — Provided by publisher.
Body text set in 11 pt Garamond
Identifiers: LCCN 2022044907 | ISBN 9781877636028 (paperback; acid-free paper)
Subjects: LCGFT: Poetry | Art | Chicano Poetry
Classification: LCC PS3553.O719 W4 2023 | DDC 811/.54 —dc23/eng/20230103
LC record available at https://lccn.loc.gov/2022044907

Acknowledgements

We would like to thank the Charles H. Kerr Publishing Company for its dedication to pro-international working-class literature. We appreciate Bella Bravo for her early copyediting and for design assembling. To bring this book to its fruition required a number of generous individuals who donated their time, expertise and encouragement: René Arceo, Cesáreo Moreno, Carlos Tortolero, current and former staff at The National Museum of Mexican Art; Pilsen activist artist Héctor Duarte who contributed the portrait of Carlos Cortéz for our cover; poet Cynthia Gallaher for proofreading, editing and encouragement throughout. Special thanks go to Fred Sasaki, Poetry Foundation, Patrick Murfin, Industrial Workers of the World Union, Chicago Branch Historian; political activist Hugh Farrell, caring professors Marc Zimmerman, Victor A. Sorell, and Robert L. Weitz who paved the way and offered inspiration. Finally, we are grateful to all living and past members of el Movimento Artistico Chicano, MARCH, Inc., Taller Mexicano de Grabado-Casa de la Cultura, Taller Mestizarte and the Chicago Mural Group, The IWW Wobblies but most of all we collectively celebrate the multi-talented Carlos Cortéz Koyokuikatl for leaving us this beautiful legacy to share. Que Viva Koyokuikatl!

—Carlos Cumpián and David Ranney, editors

Contents

II I HEAR THE FLAPPING OF WINGS

III DRAFTEES OF THE WORLD UNITE! YOU HAVE NOTHING TO LOSE BUT YOUR GENERALS!

Images

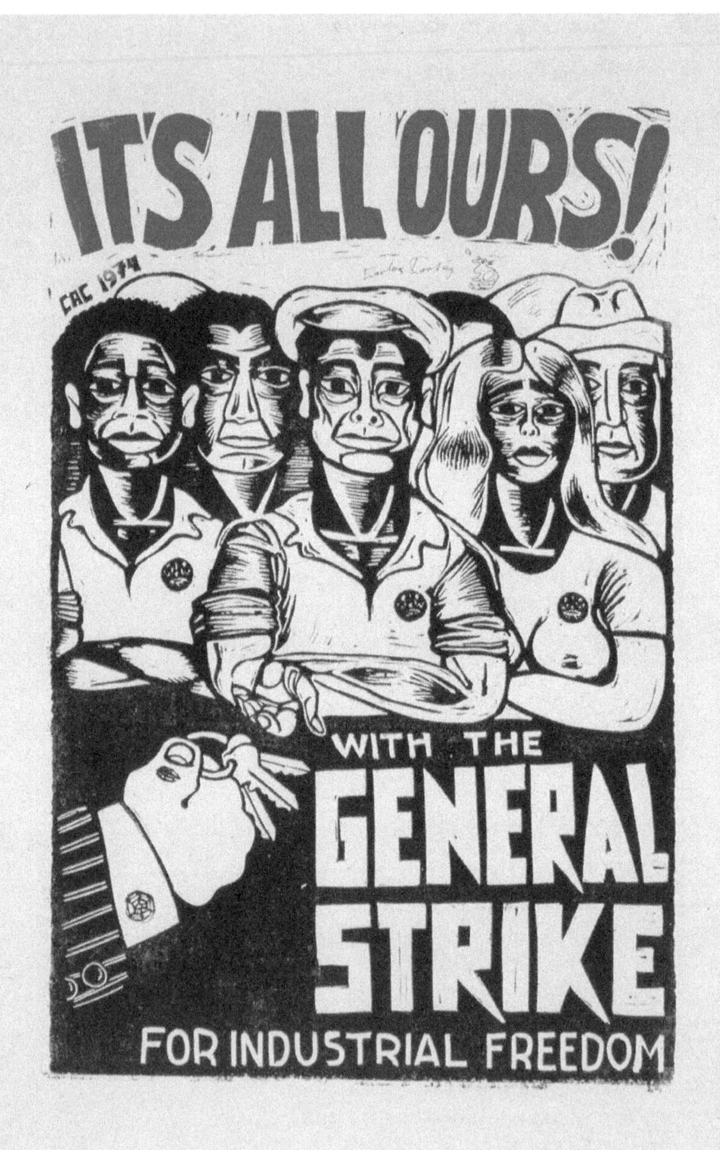

"General Strike," (1997), Permanent Collection
of the National Museum of Mexican Art.

Culture comes up from the bottom. It never comes down from the top. The only thing that comes down from the top? There is a popular Mexican saying. "Las gallinas de arriba siempre cagan en las de abajo." The chickens on the top always shit on those below.

—*Carlos Cortéz*

Carlos Cortéz (1923–2005) was born in Milwaukee, Wisconsin, to a Mexican Indian father and German mother who provided him with a multi-hyphenate, multilingual, and totally radical household. He was a singular artist of many abilities, and worked as a poet, writer, visual artist, printer, photographer, muralist, organizer, editor, and activist. We honor him today for the spellbinding life of art he created in Chicago, where he will be remembered as a beloved abuelo to generations of poets and activists.

His parents met on the street while his father was peddling copies of the Industrial Workers of the World's (IWW or "Wobblies") chief publication *Industrial Solidarity* (the newspaper changed its name to *Industrial Worker* in 1918). His mother belonged to the Socialist Party of America and wrote poetry, and his father was a Wobbly union organizer, construction worker, soap boxer, and singer—he sang in seven languages and was fluent in five.

Cortéz himself did poorly in school, "not out of lack of intelligence but lack of adhering to the academic regime." His parents called their cantankerous young son "cabeza dura" (hard head) and "dummkopf" (blockhead). And so, he decided to skip college and get to work instead. Cortéz wrote his first "serious" poem in his early twenties after being locked-up overnight on suspicion. A few years later he picked up work by the Beats and thought, "Hell, I can write this shit." When WWII broke out, he became a conscientious objector to war, stating his refusal to "shoot fellow draftees" in a "gang fight for power and wealth." He was subsequently imprisoned for eighteen months and, after his release, promptly became a lifelong member of the Industrial Workers of the World (IWW).

Often a trickster, Cortéz named himself C.C. Red Cloud, Koyokuikatl (Coyote Song), and X321826 for his many leftist columns, poems, cartoons, and etchings published in the *Industrial Worker*. And of all the names he owned during his lifetime, the name "friend" sticks the strongest. IWW member and oilfield worker Gary Cox wrote in the *Industrial Worker* newspaper: "I have never met a more gentle and honest man in my life. What you saw is what you got." A genius at living.

Young people often asked Cortéz about making a living at art—his question back to them was, "Do you want to make a living of art, or do you want to make a life of art?" In an interview with Christine Flores-Cozza he notes: "I don't turn my nose up at making money," he said, "but what is more important to me is making face."

When Cortéz bequeathed his wood and linoleum printing blocks to the National Museum of Mexican Art, he stipulated that if any of his prints became too expensive for working people to purchase, they should be used to print more and drive the price down. He used old methods to produce work and took his time to get it right. The prints embodied physical labor and provided glimpses into the love and struggles of working people and their families. Founder and president of the National Museum of Mexican Art, Carlos Tortolero commented that, "You couldn't separate the manual labor he did from who he was. Carlos was always about the real value of things. It was never money."

The primary concern of his work was the liberation of working people—"mostly the idea that we can do something with our world, particularly our human society, the way it is run, so we can better appreciate all the wealth the world has to offer." Or, as he also said: To "stop the wheels from turning."

Cortéz believed that art is essential to human experience, and therefore everyone was entitled to it.

> "My greatest goal is to feel I've turned on others to the path of creativity. Turned on others, not only to their own personal creativity, but to work toward a truly creative society. A society that is more egalitarian, more loving of each other, more recognizing of the worth in each of us."

To him, the highest praise would be for someone to say, "That's the guy who got me started. "The only thing is," he said, "you don't teach art. You open doors. It's the one thing to show you how to push an engraving tool, handle a brush, blend colors and that. But that only liberates what is already inside of you."

If you're looking for credentials, Carlos Cortéz is the author of *Where Are the Voices & Other Wobbly Poems* (1997) and *Crystal-Gazing the Amber Fluid and Other Wobbly Poems* (1990), both published by Charles H. Kerr Publishing Company, and *De Kansas a Califas & back to Chicago* (1992), published by MARCH Abrazo Press. His visual art is held at the Museum of Modern Art in New York, Smithsonian, the National Museum of Mexican Art in Chicago, and elsewhere. If you want his writing—good luck. His poems, essays, and cartoons are scarcely available in bookstores and libraries. And there is a dearth of material available online, even. So, it is our turn to carry his voice forward and encourage the next generations to take up his call for human ingenuity and solidarity. As our hero put it: "I think the best thing is that when you know something, you pass it on to the next person."

May the torch we bring here ignite something inside of you all, to carry his fire into a better future, for a better Chicago and world beyond. We need one other.

Fred Sasaki
Creative Director and Exhibition Co Curator
Poetry Magazine
Poetry Foundation

By Jay Lynch. Courtesy of the author.

In 1969, Carlos Cortéz reached me through the first poetry anthology I owned and still treasure. I paid $1.98 at a bookstore on Halsted near Armitage Street, the original Guild Books, a leftist-operated shop for *Poets of Today*, edited by Walter Lowenfels, "*85 living poets tell "how it felt to be alive in verse, since Hiroshima.*" This anthology accompanied me for a few months while traveling back and forth from my family's apartment in the Pullman/Roseland Chicago Southside neighborhood to explore the Loop and the music-friendly Northside near Lincoln Park and Old Town on weekends.

My own interest in poetry was in a nascent stage. Due to my first girlfriend's keen interest in poetry, plus that of a few high school pals who dabbled in teen angst and anti-war scribblings, I wanted to better understand poetry. Through this 143-paged-anthology, I was impressed with the single-poem entries of Gary Snyder, Charles Bukowski, Lawrence Ferlinghetti, Allen Ginsberg, Amiri Baraka, Denise Levertov, Thomas McGrath, Ishmael Reed, Alvaro Cardona-Hine, and Gregory Corso, and soon started collecting their books.

In addition, there were the lyrics to "Hard Rain's A-Gonna Fall" by Bob Dylan, which I had heard on a folk album. In a similar fashion, Cortéz' contribution was also a song, "Outa Work Blues." According to Marc Zimmerman's article in the National Museum of Mexican Art's special catalog *Carlos Cortéz Koyokuikatl: Soapbox Artist & Poet,* Cortéz', "Outa Work Blues" was included in the 1965 edition of the IWW's *Little Red Song Book*, which was widely distributed nationally and internationally, making it well known among labor activists by the time Carlos and I met.

One cool October evening in 1973, I was headed to my new second-floor apartment on the corner of Clifton and Belden when an older man wearing glasses, a thick mustache and a putty-colored slouch hat walked near me just as I started to unlock the building's door. From the sidewalk shadows, he said, "Hi, do you live here?" I was a bit startled and replied, "Yeah, I do, I just moved in last week." He quickly followed up with "Are you a 'skin?" He must have noticed my long braids and beaded design on my jacket. "What's a skin?" I asked. "An Indian, American Indian," he said.

I recall how hesitant I was to answer him, because I thought he might be some kind of government agent. I'd been part of the American

Indian ad-hoc support group in Spring 1971 that brought supplies to reclaimed Belmont Harbor at an abandoned Nike missile site. Then in October 1972, I helped house a couple of young Lakota guys at a friend's place who were on their way to the Bureau of Indian Affairs office in Washington D.C. as part of "The Trail of Broken Treaties." Between April and May 1973, I'd protested at the federal building against police repression directed against American Indian Movement members at the Pine Ridge, South Dakota Reservation at what was called "Wounded Knee Two." While these thoughts raced through my head, he moved closer to me.

My questioner followed with, "Name is Carlos Cortéz; my wife and I live on the Clifton side of this building, on the second floor." He must have also noticed my eyes open wider when he said his name. "That's funny," I said, "Carlos is my name, too." "Are you Mexican?" was his next question. I replied, "My people are native Tejanos." He seemed pleased and approached me with an outstretched hand. I let the entrance door close and put my hand out to shake his. "Okay, nice to meet you," he added. I replied, "Oralé, likewise, take it easy." Then he turned and continued to his second-floor place at 2251 N. Clifton, just a few doors down and across the street from the Oscar F. Meyer Elementary School.

I didn't realize this was the poet Carlos Cortéz from the mid-1960s' poetry anthology, and I had no idea he was an active member of the Chicago branch of the IWW. I learned all that months later. In late 1971, a fellow worker signed me up for the IWW as part of a strike for better working conditions and wages at the Mafia-dominated Hip Products warehouse on West Madison Street. Labor activist and scholar Patrick Murfin noted in the book *The IWW its First Seventy Years 1905-1975*, "The strike began during the worst sub-zero cold snap in Chicago for years. Pickets were maintained for weeks..." I confess, since the conditions were so brutal, plus being unaccustomed to Chicago's tough weather, I bailed on the strike after a month and went back to Carrizo Springs, Texas, and Southern Illinois, before returning to Chicago in April 1972.

This chance meeting with Cortéz would soon deepen my appreciation for labor's power potential—both the sold-out flabby mainstream AFL-CIO brand of unionism and the leftist American and International militant unions like IWW. I visited the Cortéz home dozens of times during the year I lived in the building for evening discussions. One time, I met some of the older guys in the union such as Fred Thompson and Patrick Murfin. I realized then that Cortéz was an essential part of the union's national monthly newspaper *Industrial Worker.* Cortéz contributed cartoons, editorials and the occasional film and book review. I found out he wrote "Outa Work Blues" after I picked up his *Little Red Songbook.* Hell, it turns out he was the backbone of their Chicago branch for a while!

He did his Wobbly activities while holding down a full-time factory job at what he called the "bubble-factory," the Richardson Company Chemical Factory. Here, he unloaded boxcars during the late 1960s and early 1970s. Cortéz made sure I never left his apartment without a pamphlet or newspaper by the Wobblies or Spain's Confederación Nacional de Trabajo (CNT), which provided news and analysis from an anarcho-syndicalist perspective. My new neighbor was, to my delight, an artist and cartoonist. He was also a poet and essayist, and a terrific polyglot joker and storyteller. He became a close friend, activist comrade, and mentor until his death in January 2005.

Cortéz' language abilities were many; he was conversationally fluent in Greek, which I witnessed as he spoke with his wife Marianna and his Greek in-laws; Italian, which he used when stopping by an old Italian shop for olive oil on Webster Street; and Spanish, with which he greeted fellow Mexican neighbors. He understood German, because his mother spoke it; he learned Spanish and some Italian from his Mexican father and had complete fluency in English since the time he was a school kid.

But how did he learn to read and recite poems in Nahuatl?[1] To answer that first I need to provide some background. "Qué Locotl!" The idea of publishing poetry in Nahuatl, español and English was practically unheard of in 1976. Yet in San Antonio, my friends Cecilio y Mia García-Camarillo brainstormed about just such a poetry contest. The goal was to select the best Chicano poems for a tri-lingual poetry book.

1 Nahuatl is an Uto-Aztecan language spoken by the peoples of central Mexico since the 7th century AD. It was the lingua franca used by indigenous cultures across Mesoamerica at the time of the Spanish invasion in 1519. Today it is spoken by nearly 1.7 million people in Mexico with smaller numbers of speakers in the U.S.

The result was an anthology *Nahuallandoing* published in Spring 1977. It became a collector's item. Cecilio and Mia's popular arts and letters Chicano monthly newsprint *Caracol* provided the perfect platform to inform raza across the nation and to send them experimental poems. Fortunately, in 1976 they asked me to spread their fliers detailing their contest and future anthology to Chicago-area poets. The first person I told and gave contest materials to was Carlos. In the work he submitted, Carlos demonstrated an innovative approach to blending and coining new words. His love poem "Tonatlancihuatl" (Shining Water Woman) appears in this book with a glossary to assist non-Nahuatl speakers. It's a shame I never recorded him reading it.

In October 1977, Salvador Alvaro Fuentes attended the joint Chicago American Indian Artist Guild and Movimiento Artistico Chicano (MARCH) cultural event that we organized. We first met at the exhibit *Anishnaabe-Waki Aztlán*, where in conversation he expressed an interest in offering Nahuatl language classes. He came across as passionate and well-informed about Nahuatl. Because I lived a few blocks from Mr. Fuentes, who also went by Aztekoyotl Ameyaltzin, he became my teacher. I was able to get fellow MARCH member Rey Vasquez to bring Cortéz who had also expressed an interest. Our trio would take notes and ask questions of Mr. Fuentes who lived in an apartment with his wife and kids who would sometimes join us for Nahuatl classes in the living room turned classroom.

By the middle of Spring 1978, we stopped taking classes mainly due to our personal schedules. My impression was Cortéz and I had become a bit better at pronouncing mainly nouns in Nahuatl. Aztekoyotl directed us to books that would deepen our appreciation of Mexico's Nahuatl culture. In the early 1980's, whenever MARCH held public poetry readings, Carlos would frequently recite from memory a poem from ancient Texcoco's past and supply translations in modern Spanish and English:

> Chalchiuitl en chayauak/Ye Xochitl ya Tlakati/Ye mokik/
> Zan tokan ya ahua Mexiko nikan moxochiuh/ Tonatimani
>
> Lluvia de esmeraldas/ Ya llegan las flores/ Es tu canción/
> cuando levantas aquí en México tus flores/ Qué fuerte el sol!

> Precious raindrops/ the flowers arrive/ this is your song/
> here in México when flowers lift up/ What strong sunlight!

I believe Carlos, having met a Nahuatl native speaker, such as Aztekoyotl, received his assistance in writing "Poema por La Dia de La Raza," which contains many Nahuatl words and is included in this colletion. The poem first appeared in his 1992 book *De Kansas a Califas & back to Chicago.*

Carlos demonstrated a sincere interest in helping Chicano youth. In 1976, I was invited by my Southside buddy and educator Guillermo Lazo to submit some poetry or artwork to a new student journal for students struggling to graduate from high school. I brought this publication's effort to Carlos' attention, and he gladly offered them five anti-war art images. All five were included in the first Latino Youth Alternative High School publication *Un Verano (One Summer).* I am sure Carlos was the oldest contributor, and he was happy to help, never expecting payment. He was always eager to help young people discover the joys of public and personal art and poetry.

In 1975, Marianna and Carlos stop paying a landlord and became homeowners. Their new place was a former general goods store, just one block west of Ashland and one block south of Diversey at 2654 N. Marshfield Street. Their main room provided good gallery space for Carlos' eclectic collection of photographs, masks, paintings and prints. Marianna and Carlos welcomed hundreds of guests over the course of their lives to enjoy the library, gallery and meeting room. Their shelves were lined with art books reflecting interests in North American and European Surrealism, German Expressionism, classical Greek, Japanese, Chinese, and Mesoamerican Indigenous art, Mexican muralism, anthropology, pop culture graphic novels, and comics including Manga. I asked him what led to his interest in all these Japanese-related magazines and haiku journals. With a twinkle in his eye, he said that he'd dated a Japanese woman before he married Marianna, and she made an impression on him.

Carlos' front room also held an ever-growing collection of poetry and fiction of his favorites: Kenneth Rexroth, Kenneth Patchen, William Carlos Williams, Carl Sandburg, Langston Hughes, Octavio Paz, Walt Whitman, Robert Burns, Cavafy, Joel Climenhaga, Edward

Abbey, Jack London and Kerouac. There were various published Black, American Indian, Chicano and Puerto Rican poets he came to know in person and read on stage with them such as Michael Warr, Dennis Brutus, Joffre Stewart, Simon J. Ortiz, Lonnie Poco, E. Donald Two-Rivers ("Eddie"), Ana Castillo, Lorna Dee Cervantes, Sandra Cisneros, Abelardo "Lalo" Delgado, José Montoya, Trinidad Sanchez Jr. Raúl Niño, Beatriz Badikian-Gartler, Cynthia Gallaher, Luis J. Rodriguez, Frank Varela and David Hernandez.

Carlos drew inspiration from listening to music, mainly classical works and some folkloric collections from Mexico and South America. For example, when Chicago's classical music station WFMT offered its listeners a daylong special review of German composer Johannes Brahms, Cortéz would take that day off from work or his volunteer assignments. He disconnected his wall telephone, got comfortable on the sofa, and assembled his pack of French Gitanes, German Roth-Händle or Mexican Faros, an ashtray, lighter, his footstool and a cup of black expresso, along with a tall glass of ice water. Once the program started, there was no talking, and he would close his eyes and listen to every note. Marianna and Carlos would on occasion attend operas at Chicago's Civic Opera House. He didn't care about pop or contemporary rock but enjoyed Mexican ballads and corridos when entertaining a crowd. He also relished Sundays when he was able make it to Maxwell Street's "Flea Market" to listen to live Blues musicians.

Cortéz became active in 1975 with MARCH, founded by José G. Gonzalez (1933-2022) and Efrain Martinez. He jumped at the chance to help promote their photography exhibit of Augustin V. Casasola who recorded the earliest clashes of the 1910-1917 Revolution. Cortéz designed a linocut poster of men and women peasant revolutionary Zapatistas for the exhibit *Mexposicion 2* held at the University of Illinois, Chicago. This was the first poster I had seen by Cortéz with a Mexican theme. José G. Gonzalez designed a standard photography advertisement for the same event.

Carlos was inspired by this exhibit and soon followed up with a large linocut profile of a mustached campesino in a sombrero. It became one of his most popular pieces on display at our joint Chicago American Indian Artists Guild and MARCH exhibition, the first in a series of Anishinaabe Waki-Aztlan exhibits in Illinois. It was Cortéz who invited me to join this modest arts nonprofit and contribute to its journal *Abrazo*, which became our first in a series of collaborations as cultural workers. In the first issue of *Abrazo*, Cortéz developed a column called "El Machetazo" (The Machete Hit), which was critical of private art galleries and most museums' elitist atmosphere and hours. In the second issue of summer 1979, his sweeping narrative poem "*This is The Land*" was published.

Cortéz quickly became my literary role model. His confidence rubbed off on me and other young Chicanos. We too felt our voices and talents could be of some value. Consider this passage from his first "El Machetazo" column articulating in no uncertain terms his politics:

> In these days of rising liberation movements, another priority should be the liberation of art. Free it from those who use it as another means of differentiating themselves from those who are of the 'lowah classes' and bring it back to where it originated and where it belongs, among the people. For that I like graphics and murals...murals are beautiful. They are out in the open for all to see and be accepted by the people, you can't take a wall and cart it off to some rich bitch's mansion or yacht.

Nearly twenty years later in 1995, my son Camilo Cumpián, age 19, studied a poster by Cortéz and recreated it as a block-long mural along Milwaukee Avenue near the Logan Square's CTA station. Towering black and red images of defiant marchers from Cortéz' "La Lucha Continúa!" greeted drivers and pedestrians. Clearly, there have been several Chicano Mexicano, Central and South American artists who were his colleagues in Pilsen and paid homage to Carlos Cortéz Koyokuikatl by making silkscreen graphics, such as those of multitalented René Arceo or painted big canvasses rendered by Hector Duarte. Other artists have made Carlos Cortéz Koyokuikatl their subject like that of highly accomplished engraver and printmaker Carlos Barreren's 2015 "Koyokuikatl." I recall it was Pilsen muralist Aurelio Diaz Tekpankalli who first painted Cortéz' visage in 1982. Pilsen artist and Chicago Public School art teacher Francisco Mendoza and mural tour guide and labor activist José Guerrero also painted Cortéz. The most famous photo of Cortéz was taken in a posed studio setting. It was by

Columbia College graduate Alex Sunheart Galindo. I am sure there are others that have made and will make Cortéz-inspired art.

Those who knew him would say Cortéz was this cultured, mature man who did not put on airs or take the position as some judgmental professor or boss. Rather, he really cared about doing serious projects however humble the budget or materials. Cortéz helped many working class or marginalized human beings see the value of self-expression and self-affirmation.

Professor Marc Zimmerman wrote in *Chicano Writers, Third Series of the Dictionary of Literary Biography*, "While Carlos Cortéz may ultimately be better remembered for his linocuts and woodcut graphics than for his verse, he exhibits some of the same virtues in the visual and verbal media; it may indeed be said that in some ways Cortéz translates radical Mexican traditions into populist verse. His graphics, often augmented with words, are striking, bold and direct, as are his poems." In an unpublished January 1988 interview, Carlos Cortéz said, "The social forces of repression and the consequent forces of rebellion have long influenced my writing as well as...other forms of expression."

I close with a quote from the foreword Cortéz wrote in the chapbook, *The Age of Pollution* (A Transient Book, 1990) for his long-time friend and traveling companion Joel Climenhaga. "Like any artist, a writer of poetry strips one's self naked before the world. A poet may put on a different colored wig or sport a false mustache, but the true person always comes through, eventually." To that I say we are getting in this book the real Carlos Cortéz Koyokuikatl in both images and heightened language of poetry. I recall on numerous occasions when asked why he was a poet as well as an artist Cortéz would calmly reply, "Poetry is the least prostituted of the arts. It rarely has been subjugated to the wishes of capital."

Sí, La Lucha Continúa,

Carlos Cumpián
Poet, teacher and co-editor

"Braceros," (ca, 1970s), Permanent Collection
of the National Museum of Mexican Art.

"El Dia de la Raza" (1992), Scratchboard, From: *de Kansas a Califas & Back to Chicago: Poems and Art*, MARCH Abrazo Press, 1992. P. 49.

I

MAGICALLY TRANSFORMED BY LAUGHING CHILDREN

Progress

Roaring jets
fill the sky
that once echoed
with the song of birds.

Flashing neons
shine on streets
that once shone
beneath moon and stars.

Asphalt and concrete
smother the good dirt
that once nurtured
soft cool grass.

Open windows
that once let in
the song of crickets
regurgitate with the howl
of TV loudspeakers
chanting the way of mediocrity
to the cellmate multitudes
as the crickets silently go
someplace else.

Roadways once lined
with weeds and flowers
are festooned
with motels and billboards,
old papers and broken bottles,
cigar butts and drive-ins,
Kleenex and step-ins,
empty beer cans
and empty car shops,

and certain discarded objects
that cause the cardinals
no small indignation,
as flowers silently grow
someplace else.

With its banana splits
and split atoms,
quiz shows and loan offices,
juke boxes and supermarkets,
nuclear tests and piece-work,
best-sellers and marriage counselors,
formulas and falsies,
progress goes on
and on and
on and
on
thru
quickly-built subdivisions
and chrome-plated
shopping centers,
hacking its way
thru the neon jungle
leaving farther behind
the spot on the road
where the wrong fork
was taken.

J.B.
(Jukebox)

Him alla time make noise
Him neva eat hamburgers
Him neva drink beer
    Him just gulp down
        Nickels
        & Dimes
        & Quarters
Him sing alla time
Him sing Hillbilly music
Him sing rock 'n' roll
Him sing Tin Pan Alley
Him sing Hollywood
Him blow polka
Him alla time make
    Helluva racket
Him neva shut up
    But
    Ho Boy!
Him neva do commercials.

Purification 1

Covering rooftops
rail yards and coal piles,
even cemeteries
and squat supermarket roofs,
for once the city looks
beautiful.

Question

You with the big bright eyes
and lips that are only meant to
touch lollypops;
Locks of hair that never stay in
place
and scuffed-up shoes and
dirty knees;
No, little termite, parked cars
and dark lanes
are not for you quite yet.

You have to learn of this World
that your elders have brought
you into;
a World that would be much
better off
if it were put into your grubby
little hands
at the mercy of your mischievous
twinkle.

Must you too someday have to
look upon
another pair of innocent eyes,
lollypop lips and dirty knees
and ask yourself this same
agonizing question?

Windy City Christmas

In a chilly alleyway
off West Madison Street,
Santa Claus is an old man
with a dirty beard
passing a bottle of cheap
Muscatel
to his buddies

Efficiency

The right amount of snow
with the right amount of wind
plus, the foresighted wisdom
of our city fathers
can sure louse up
a civilization.

Invasion

We have been invaded!
By a Monster!
Not from Russia
Not from Outer Space,
But it is here
In every living room!
Holding us in its power,
Sapping our will,
Breaking down all resistance
To its
LONE CYCLOPTIC
EYE

Communication

So often have I listened to those cultural snobs
who consider themselves authorities on music,
wax profoundly
on the works of Bach
and the complexity
of his compositions
that can only be understood
by musicians' musicians
and certainly beyond
the comprehension
or appreciation
of the unschooled
rabble.

But I remember a bygone evening as I was spinning
my hi-fi Brandenburg Concerto on my low-fi machine
from the kitchen
the voice of my Mother
who spent most of her life
in a German farm community
never digging anything
more uplifting than
a wheezy Saturday night
Concertina,
asking me:
"Son, what are you playing there that sounds so much
like springtime?"

Youngstown

The waters of the Mahoning
are being hidden
by a jungle of steel mills
spreading like a rusty
        scab
on the Ohio landscape.

A once beautiful valley
and its grey-pallid
        hillsides
speak out
with a lesson on
        Free Enterprise
no textbook could give.

Requiem for a Street*

Well, they have finally gotten around to the street. The apostles of civic improvement are advancing with their cranes and bulldozers, tearing down the old slums so that newer and bigger and loftier slums can be built on this. The street was once lined with an endless array of small shops, bistros and hole-in-the-wall restaurants where one could bask in the culinary delights of faraway places, where one could walk by small music stores and hear strange music that somehow was not strange at all. Where the sidewalk passersby would be constantly beset by sidewalk pitchmen and Gypsy fortune tellers.

And where else in this standardized American metropolis could you hear of the wonderful quality and ridiculously low price of the latest fashion in suits extolled to you in Spanish with a Yiddish accent, or the Gypsy girls who take one quick size-up and start handing you their line in the tongue of your ancestors?

It was not the cleanest of streets, not here in this unclean city. But it was a happy street, happy with the smell of pizza, roasted lamb heads, Turkish coffee, and tacos; happy with the raucous babble of many voices; happy with the voices from the ghettos of Bucaresti, Odessa and Wilno; happy with the voices from Piraeus, Salonika and Plaka; happy with the voices of those who had known only the roof of Romanian, Hungarian and Serbian skies; happy with the voices from Morelia, Ixtapalapa and Nuevo Laredo; happy with the voices from Caguas, Ponce and Arecibo; yes, happy with the voices from Mobile, Beaumont and Chattanooga; happy with the voices from Palermo, Catania and Livorno, a small united nations that somehow wasn't completely united and somehow it didn't make too much difference.

True, it was quite a din but it was a human din, it was a mess but it was a human mess, not like the din that is heard on the street now; the mechanical roar of the cranes and mechanical thump of the large ball and mechanical roar of the bulldozers directed from distant offices, committees and kickback artists with mechanical mentalities and mechanical hearts, and in the wake of the redevelopment juggernaut leaving behind a mess that would put a B-29 to shame.

The rubble creeps up on the last remaining pawnshops, bodegas and pizzerias, the last remaining small haberdasheries, kafenios and taquerias. Street of zucchini, baklava and enchilada, at last you are falling before the advance of standardization; street of olives, snails and avocados, your days are numbered; street of chianti, mazel and retsina, of ouzo, arak and tequila with your guitar thumping cantinas and belly-dancing tavernas. Those who do not know you have the power to destroy you, for behold, advancing in the distance following in the wake of the bulldozers and rising above the clouds of dust of your corpse are your brand-new tombstones called civic redevelopment. Human anthills look like a combination of cell-block and skyscraper. Yes, they are building bigger and better tenements destined to become bigger and blighter areas.

And you, you good city planners and your fat pocket contractors, when your job is completed and you come down here to look at your accomplishments, are you honestly going to believe you've made any improvements other than in the health of your back pockets?

**A stretch of Chicago's Halsted Street between Roosevelt Road and Greek Town was destroyed in the late 1950s/early 1960s to make room for the University of Illinois and the Congress Expressway.*

Sisters Beneath the Concrete

I have never been on the streets of Prague,
But I know our cities are sisters;
I have never seen Soviet tanks on the streets of Prague,
But I have seen National Guard tanks on Chicago streets.
I have not witnessed the heads of young people
Being crushed on the streets of Prague,
But I have witnessed the heads of young and old people
Being clubbed on the streets of Chicago,
And I have savored the unpleasant flavor of tear gas
On my palate, and there is no doubt in my mind that
Our cities are sisters!

When the clubs of repression come down on the heads
Of freedom-seekers,
Be it in Prague, Chicago, Soweto,
Warsaw, Beijing or Tlatelolco,
There is no doubt in my mind:
All cities are sisters!
Whenever people stand up
For what is justice to them
And forces of repression
Seek to throttle their voices,
All people are each other's brothers and sisters
And the cities where they live
Are indeed sisters!

Two generations ago when the forces of repression
Wiped out the town of Lidice,
Bulldozing all traces beneath the good Slavic soil,
Thinking that such a deed
That Lidice would forever be interred,
But Lidice rose again
On the streets of Prague
And on the streets of Chicago—

Yes—on the streets of Tlatelolco and Beijing;
On streets too numerous to mention,
Where linger yet the bloodstains of those nameless
But unforgotten ones,
Who have consigned their oppressors
To the eventual oblivion
They so richly deserve!

Geography is but a chronicle of distances
And nation is but a word;
The differences of skin and tongue
Are but delectable condiments
On a well-cooked repast!
Prague—Chicago—
Sisters in spirit and in the flesh,
May you and all your other sisters
Stand forever as monuments
To the follies and hopes
Of our kind!

City of Angels

Like a malignant behemoth amoeba,
Emerging from the ocean
Spreading across valleys
And over mountains
Corroding the landscape
With its population
Explosion;
Home of the Skid Row Bum
Plodding his streets
In a downtown that makes
Chi's Loop seem clean,
A real Oakie town
Where white-robed salvationists
Fleece their flocks
In architectural monstrosities
Called Temples of Everlasting
Mystic Revelation;
Where oil refinery smoke stacks
And a million exhaust pipes
Roaring down the freeways
Permeate the sea breeze
With Free Enterprise excrement
Begetting a bastard child
That floats over rooftops
Toward the mountains
And failing to climb over
Comes back to creep
Into the laundry
Of a million housewives
And
In the Food dishes
Of a million puppy dogs
And

Into the watery eyelids
    Of a million workingmen
Driving down endless Freeway
Caravan subterranean parking
Lot high rent eternity
    Wistfully gazing toward
The other side of the ridge
    Where
    Free from the Grey Imminence
In suburban palaces live
    Cinematic courtesans, Real
    Estate Brokers, automobile
    salesmen, and refinery
    owners
Who gaze back down hoping Man will
    Never learn
    To advance with his technology.

The Last Expressway

In musty old books that are to be found
in the few libraries that remain
can be seen pictures of trees.

It is said that there were many trees
in the days before the land was covered
by one-hundred-story apartment houses.

In days before the final great war
when the Russians licked the Americans
or the Americans licked the Russians
or the Chinese licked them both,
no one seems to remember
since most libraries have been replaced
by one-hundred-story apartment houses.

The construction crews are going to tear up
the last expressway to make room for
more one-hundred-story apartment houses.

The last expressway is twenty-five
thousand miles long
but has nowhere to go.

Three Spirits: Frank Little, Wesley Everett, Joe Hill

From the wide-belted wind-swept plains
where the imperceptible sobs of the dead tribesmen
are lost on the ears of the speeding motorist
bound on his way toward some intangible oblivion

And over the hump-backed backbone of a continent
whose deep-throated canyons and serpentine
roadways
are a strain on the nerves of the speeding motorist
bound on his way toward some intangible oblivion

To the salt-sprayed meadows and tall evergreen forests
whose rocky-shored ocean is only another obstacle
in the path of the speeding motorist
bound on his way toward some intangible oblivion

The shadows of all the long-gone spirits drift endlessly
unnoticed by those who are destined to become
spirits
but notice everything including the speeding
motorist
bound on his way toward some intangible oblivion

And occasionally these spirits stop drifting
long enough to come together in small groups
to reminisce of days gone by before they
become part of the spirit world

And somewhere on a high scrub-timbered mountain
slope
overlooking a sprawling, growing West-country
metropolis

"Yosemite Night Scene" (1992), Scratchboard, From: *de Kansas a Califas & Back to Chicago: Poems and Art*, MARCH Abrazo Press, 1992. P. 20-21.

II

I HEAR THE FLAPPING OF WINGS

Adios Tecopita

(News item: The Tecopa pupfish was removed from the U.S. government's list of endangered species because it has become extinct. The one-and-a-half-inch fish is the first species ever removed from the list for that reason. Interior Department officials said they took the action after their search of 40 waterways around Tecopa, California failed to turn up any of the fish in 1982.)

There are no more pupfish in the waterways
Around Tecopa,
The town they were named after;
That is what they tell us,
Those officials who keep track of
Things like that; what sadness,
A whole race of creatures has disappeared
Never to come back again!
It is said that the big fish always eat
The little fish, and that seems to be
The morality of today's world
Only the big fish who did in the Tecopa
Pupfish do not have scales, gills or fins
Nor do they live under water.
It gives me a sadness
that a whole race of
Creatures has disappeared—never to come back.
the buffalo, they had meat and hides
and were in the invader's way,
that is why they no longer darken the Plains,
but these little pup fish,
    What meat did they have?
    What hides did they offer?
And whose way were they in?

I have never seen these fish that were only
an inch-and-a-half long nor have I ever
had a frying pan that was only two inches wide
so, I would never have bothered them.

Anyway, a whole race of creatures has disappeared
Never to come back again.
I used to swim in small rivers and lakes
and at the same time drink of the water.
I no longer drink the water
while I swim,
and at many waters it is not
even safe to swim;
one river
even caught fire
while flowing through a city.

I used to see flocks of antelope
from the bus window.
Now I must go to a zoo
to get that close to an antelope
it's the same with the buffalo.

I enjoy the Sun
when rising in the morning ... East
and when setting in the evening ...West
because these are the times when
I can look him straight
in the face without hurting my eyes.

But now there are places where I can do
the same at high noon;
it gives me a sadness
that a whole race of
creatures have disappeared
never to come back again ...

Did you know about the Tecopa fish
as you raced down
the highways throwing beer cans
out of your windows?
When you turn up your
air conditioners, hair dryers,
and electric toothbrushes
or when your thermostats are up high
as you can walk around in shorts
while looking at the snowdrifts outside,
or when you are making
tracks with your snowmobiles?
Do you even care
that from the face of this earth
a whole race of creatures has disappeared
never to come back again?
It gives me a sadness.

"Centinela" (1992), Scratchboard, From: *de Kansas a Califas & Back to Chicago: Poems and Art*, MARCH/Abrazo Press, 1992. P. 36-37.

Las Calandrias

In the Plazuela en El Paso
The trees are loaded
With warbling fruit.

Every now and then
All this singing fruit
Explodes into the sky.

To load down yet another tree.

Purification 2

The street of one-story
suburban ranch type homes
and their equally conforming
naked lawn plots

Are magically transformed
by laughing children
every afternoon
at the sound of the
last school bell.

Science Fiction Story

Two brave spacemen
sailing
a disk-shaped
chariot
far from their own
galaxy
found a small green
planet,
swooped down to
observe
the scene below,
shuddered,
and sailed back
home

Ersatz

On a cloudy night
a string of blinking
ten-watt bulbs
advertising
Frank's Gas and Oil
substitutes for the stars.

Sun Chant

Driving down endless
freeway miles of Free
Enterprise desolation
the motorists do not know
a flock of birds fly overhead
or do they care.

Only a group of small boys
standing upon the embankment
and flying their kites
know there is a Universe.

The Bugs

When the dinosaurs first trod the antediluvian Earth
They were here watching
and being careful not to be stepped upon.

And when those reptilian behemoths
perished in the face of the holocaust
of the growing pains of an infant Earth
They were here feasting on their corpses.

When the first mammals made their timid debut
They were here nesting in their fur
and burrowing in their skin.

And when a strange new creature walking on two legs
came out of the trees to build his cities
They were here burrowing between the stone and wood
and luxuriating in his kitchens and sewers.

They were here thriving on smog,
thriving in polluted waterways
and thriving on insecticides and DDT,
thriving in soot-blackened cities
and drought-whitened country sides;
They only looked on with mild interest
as the mushroom clouds began to sprout.
They are still here.
but where is man, where is man, WHERE IS MAN?!?!

"Tehachapi Pass" (1992), Scratchboard, From: *de Kansas a Califas & Back to Chicago: Poems and Art,* MARCH Abrazo Press, 1992. P. 17.

Tehachapi Pass

You used to be able to see
the Mountains on the other side
of the Valley ...
but now you long
for the clean Desert air
as you watch the smog
drifting up from Los Angeles.

I hear the flapping of wings;
the California Condor is coming back,
even if he has to migrate
from Machu Picchu!

Calabria

In the early morning
Mediterranean mists
a turbulent tidal wave
of mountains
bears down
on the dwarfed
ocean liner.

The Buzz of the Flies Grows Louder

A small nit opens up
Disgorging a squirming
White maggot
And the buzz of the flies grows louder.
On the shores of a lake
Grows a creeping slime
Through which gasping fish
Throw themselves on a soiled shore to die
And the excrement of mismanaged factories
Changes the water's blue
To a murky brown
And the buzz of the flies grows louder.
In a steamy jungle
Far from home and family
And sick with fever
A young man looks blankly
At the gore running from his open wound
While the pulse of life
Slips slowly from his painful body
And the buzz of the flies grows louder.
In a far-off city
Far from their homes and families
A group of old men
Argue about the shape of a table
And the buzz of the flies grows louder.
And in another city
Far from their homes
But with their families
Well-dressed people,
In spite of the drenching rain
Gather in ballrooms
Too crowded for dancing
To eagerly welcome their new chief
And the buzz of the flies grows louder.

And in yet another city,
On his banner-draped balcony
Where his adoring multitudes
Can gaze upon him as they express
Their everlasting fealty
As he exhorts them
To follow the only true goals
And the buzz of the flies grows louder.
High up in an armored capsule
Far from home, family and planet
The astronaut for the first time
Looks closely upon another planet,
Gazing at its mystery
Then shifts his eyes
Toward the direction of his home planet,
Gazing with fascination
As it reminds him of his old classroom globe,
So remote that he cannot imagine,
Much less see
The wars, poverty, misery and hopes
Of his own kind down there
And the buzz of the flies grows louder.
And again, another nit opens up
Disgorging another squirming
White maggot
And the buzz of the flies
Grows louder and louder

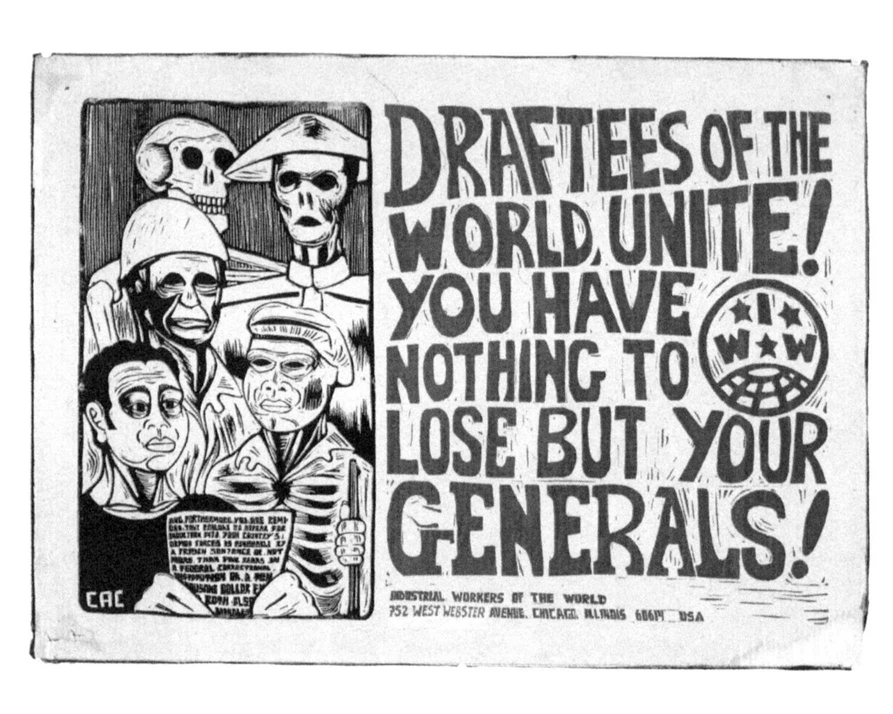

"Draftees of the World Unite! You Have Nothing to Lose But Your Generals!" (ca, 1964/1969-early 1970s), Permanent Collection of the National Museum of Mexican Art.

III

DRAFTEES OF THE WORLD UNITE! YOU HAVE NOTHING TO LOSE BUT YOUR GENERALS

Ba-Gia Requiem for a Village

The wailing of women and the stench of corpses
permeate the once peaceful forests and rice paddies,
in the wake of a benevolent liberating army
in their pursuit of an elusive enemy,
in the long war where nobody loses
except the people.

The once peaceful village
has become a smoldering tomb
of bombed-out stucco and splintered bamboo
and stilled children who will never be noisy again,
as the liberating army moves on to yet undestroyed villages
in the long-stalemated war where nobody loses
except the people.

A baby futilely sucks away on the breast of his dead mother,
as the pulse of life starts slowly slipping from his body,
while only a distance away with equal futility
a mother puts her breast in the mouth of her dead baby,
as the pulse of reason starts slowly slipping from her mind.

On the half-hanging door of a burnt-out home
still hangs the wedding decorations
now scorched by fire,
while on the floor lies a can of cooking oil
marked, "Donated by the people
of the United States of America,"
and next to the can of cooking oil,
the bride herself, her head blown open from a shell
donated by the people of the United States of America.

The tow-headed young soldier
who only months before felt a twinge of remorse,
at having shot an unarmed civilian in the back,
after weeks and after months of seeing more
dead women and children than dead
Viet Cong guerrillas,
looks down on the face and body
of a budding young girl,
no longer wondering if she died
from a bullet he fired,
but only thinking what a gorgeous lay
if she were still alive,
and only dimly aware that his own personal
predicament has been
donated by the people of the United States of America
as he continues to play his own little role
In this long exasperating war where nobody loses
except the people.

The bombed-out schoolhouse with its
smoldering little corpses
stands out in mute testimony and roaring indictment
of a civilization's history that is replete with the festering
of "man's inhumanity to man" in this incidental phase
of a long stupid war where nobody loses
except the people.

Newsmen no longer direct their attention only
to the atrocities of the other side,
as they unabashedly record the ruin and the desolation
so, you in your armchair can follow the progress
of a long stupid stalemated war where nobody loses
except the people.

Yes, you, you comfortable people,
an ocean and a continent away in your
comfortable unbombed homes,
be they air-conditioned split-level suburban,
or stuffy four-room garbage-smelly
bitch-at-the-landlord urban,
when your children come home
from their unbombed schools,
and are finally tucked away
in their unbombed bedrooms,
and you take one last look at the television news
in your unbombed living room, is Ba Gia
just another strange sounding name
from a faraway war that is just another goddamn
long stupid war where
nobody loses except the people?

Apres-Midi D'un Jet

It was a hot afternoon
    at Lincoln Park Zoo
and the smell of animal dung
    sweaty people and
cooking hot dogs curdled the air.

Further down the lake there were
    maneuvers
and goose-formatted trios of jets
    roaring flew overhead
perverting the blue sky with
    their smoke tridents.

One show-off jet nose-dived
    low over the zoo
disturbing animals, shaking tree
    leaves and causing
frightened little children to clasp
    their hands
over their ears.

A tall blond young father
taking his boy to the kiddie train
angrily snarled, "I hope they send
    that bastard to Viet Nam!"

A short dark little oriental woman
    with her two tiny sons
and one tiny daughter looked up
    briefly,
and as if to herself
    said,
    "I hope they don't!"

The Aliens

The first world war killed quite a few people
and the second world war
killed off a few more,
but the third world war made the first two
look like Sunday school picnics
and there was hardly anyone left
after the fourth.

The fifth world war never got started because
it was then that the Aliens began to show up.
No one knew where they came from
& how they landed.

In fact, little was known of them
except that they were different, repulsive,
and did not belong in this world.
Surrounded by Aliens, the world decided
to fight no more.

An eager young husband
rushed home to his young wife
who was having the first birth since War number 4,
only to find she had given birth to an Alien.
Fuming with rage, he pulled out his gun
and aimed it at her
but she whispered feebly, "Wait"

Then she turned the creature over
to show him
a birthmark.
Slowly the young husband aimed
the gun on himself and pulled the trigger.

Ballad of a Draftee

He didn't know what it was all about,
just out of school, no job, nowhere to go
or anything to go with, when the Board
told him he was going to travel far.

Naturally he was thrilled.
With his spanking new uniform
and shiny new gun he got on the big boat
and began to see "The World."

Months later in a steamy-hot
miserable jungle,
sweat pouring down his face
and his crotch full of lice.

He still didn't know what it was all about
or could he understand why these people
whose freedom he was sent to protect
were shooting at him.

When he felt the impact of the bullet
in his last split second of consciousness
he began to wonder.

(1964)

Houn' Dog

Trotting along the sidewalk
with not a feline in sight
to give chase to
and not a girl doggie in sight
that he can pursue
but just the same as happy as
only a houn' dog can be,
he spies the recruiting poster
in front of the post office.

His tail stops wagging
long enough,
as he cranes his head forward
to make the sniff test
and upon seeing that it
does not sniff too well,
with excellent body English
and a back paw salute,
he administers upon this artifact
of an alleged higher creation,
his most eloquent appraisal.

Careful How You Cast That Stone

Who is responsible for the wasted lands,
the bombed-out cities
and disease-ridden children?
Upon whose shoulders lay this guilt?
Who are these villains who send young men
to fertilize the battlefield grasses
and reap a harvest of weeping women?

Who are these miscreants
responsible for the murder
of potential artists, future scientists
and productive working men?
Who are these abortionists
of human progress?

Is it the rich men alone,
wealthy beyond their own need
who owns factories
where implements of human
destruction are made,
whose existence depends
upon men destroying men?

Is it the politicians securely
ensconced in legislative chambers,
who with a flourish of a pen and with
the money-laden handshake of the rich men
who play with the lives of millions
with less concern than a chess player
for his chessmen,
(These living chessmen are ALL pawns)
whose very existence depends
upon men hating men?

Is it the ego-strutting generals
resplendent in their monkey suits
and blood-bought campaign ribbons,
each ribbon and medal
representing countless hosts
of broken families and shattered futures,
who mortally fear the PEACE
that would render them useless citizens,
whose very existence depends
upon men killing men?

But is this unholy trinity the true culprit,
these misanthropes of Man's evolution?
These rich men whose wealth make them
powers without question,
from whom and whence do they get
such unearned wealth?

Their miserable little pimps,
bemedaled gnats of the battlefield
and pompous maggots
of the legislative chamber pots.

Who permits them their uncontested power?
Who grants them the privilege to rule?
Upon whose shoulders lay this guilt?
You fellow workers
as you stand before a mirror
ask YOURSELF that question!

"Welcome Home" (2000), The Permanent Collection
of the National Museum of Mexican Art.

North Shore Line Interlude

They came into the car
        I was riding
these two naval officers and
        their two prisoners
who were just a couple
        of lads
that after three years
        found they no longer
cared for the navy blue
        and these officers
had them sit in the seat
        facing me
while they found themselves
        a roomier seat
across the aisle
        where they could
small-talk their way back to
        the naval station
in comfort
        and as I sat talking
and smoking with these kids
        I asked, "Fellas,
try and hide those handcuffs,
        I don't want anybody
to think *I'm* the cop!"

Peace Walkers

Walking,
walking in spite of the taunts of the conformists
and the indifferent stares of the apathetic.

Walking
because somehow, they no longer rely on their
congressmen
and appeals to the highest office.

Walking,
because among other things,
in the summer of nineteen-forty-five a horrible
new child was born
on the sandy wastes of New Mexico
and a short time later displayed its horror
on two human cities.

Walking in the hopes of removing the apathy from
those stares
and the conformity from those conformists.

Walking,
because the walking they do today
IS ONE LESS WALK
THEIR CHILDREN WILL HAVE TO DO.

America Your Face Is Dirty

When your bomb fell
more had fallen
than just a bomb

When you destroyed a city
more was destroyed
than just a city

When you killed thousands
in one searing flash
more was lost
than just human lives

Among those survivors you left
are those who will bear
the rest of their days
gruesome scars
almost as gruesome
as your own invisible
scar

You
O' Great Beautiful
Bargain Counter Democracy,
ever vigilant against
foreign ideology
making sure
your
great light
shines upon all
can you ever wipe from
your face the blood
of
HIROSHIMA!!!

The Day of the Pika-Don

One beautiful August day
Miyako-San went out shopping
and instead of buying herself
    another kimono
she bought a western dress.
"Āh so," she giggled as she
    admired
the strange unfamiliar patterns,
"Now I, too, can be a modern girl."

Happily, she walked down the
    street
unmindful of the disapproving
    glances
of the old conservatives
and ever conscious of those who
    turned their heads
at the gay print dress that did
    not conceal
her swaying hips or jiggling
    bosom.
her walk was interrupted by a
    blinding flash.

Weeks later she woke up in an
emergency hospital
miraculously alive and in one
    piece
but her western dress had been
completely destroyed.

On her alabaster body was etched
    forever
the strange unfamiliar western
    design,
burnt in forever for any future
    lover to admire.

When she learned the full story
he made a vow never to
    again, to put on
any western clothing.

What Happened to Armistice Day?

Perhaps a Gold Star can soothe a mother's aching heart
and give solace to a father's broken dreams.

Perhaps a Gold Star can bring home the bacon,
be a companion to a widowed young wife
and lie at night between her yearning loins to stifle nocturnal sobs.

Perhaps a Gold Star can be a good pal
to those orphaned kids and play with them
in the evening and drive them to school in the morning,
as they await their time to audition for Gold Stars of their own.

Perhaps a Gold Star can proliferate
and multiply until there are so damn many
that Fort Knox will be just another hole
in the ground and the parasites
can have a real ball pointing with pride.

But I don't think y'oughta worry too much about Gold Stars anymore.

You see—

War is being automated!

Athens, May 1, '66

We asked the priest for the grave of *Lambrakis*[1]
but he pointed us in the opposite direction.

Later when we finally found
the simple concrete shaft
decorated with the CNVA[2] symbol
instead of the cross, we remembered
the annoyance on the priest's face.

Naturally now, we will warn all our friends
but we will also instruct them
to always ask the priest.

1 Grigoris Lambrakis (Greek: Born April 3, 1912-May 27, 1963) was a Greek politician, physician, track and field athlete, member of the University of Athens School of Medicine. He was in the Greek Resistance fighting Nazis during WW2; he later became a leading anti-war activist. He was killed by far-Right terrorists which provoked mass protests and led to a political crisis.

2 Committee for Non-Violent Action, an anarchist-inclined direct action pacifist group active in the 1960s.

Sunday On Manitowoc Ave.

The morning sound of birds
is noisily interrupted
by the passing over
of Brave New Frontiers,
spanking new jets
joined by a bit of obligato
from the church bells.

After a little while
the birds can be heard again.

Then You Can Wish Me 'Happy New Year!'

What are you all so damn gay about?
        With your tinseled noisemakers
        funny hats
        and nervously relaxed
        inhibitions.
Just because it's the last hour
of the last night
        of the last day
                        of the last week
                                        of the last month
                                                        of the year;
just because at this particular time
the joints stay open all night,
the lid's way off, you can get real gay,
drunker than a hoot owl
and nobody gives a hoot,
if you pinch somebody else's wife
or your wife rubs herself against
somebody else's husband
because somehow this is a real special
occasion where you can yip it up
while working on a two-day hangover
waiting for the stroke of midnight
when everybody wishes everybody else
the felicitations of another 365 days
like was done exactly a year ago
to the very minute and many times before
and be done exactly a year from now
to the very minute and many times more (we hope).

You there, fellow-working stiff
happy as a lark with your overtime paychecks
paying off your air-conditioned mortgage
and wondering why you have such a hard time

laying aside that nest egg,
when you tell me
that you're not going to make
any more shell casings
or help manufacture any other lethal objects
to be used against members of your own class,
then you can wish me
"Happy New Year!"

You there, bright young college graduate
with your Master's degree in science
and your top security laboratory job
liberal mindedly joining committees
to promote peace and understanding,
when you tell me that you will no
longer use your great brain
to help turn out more potent missiles,
but with your scientific background
wise up us dumb jerks to the real situation
and its far-reaching consequences,
that we might organize ourselves
before it's too damn late,
then you can wish me
"Happy New Year!"

You there, little schoolmarm
so prim and petite
in your starched white blouse
indoctrinating your wide-eyed little charges,
dressing up the miseries and bloodbaths
of mankind's mistakes
as great valorous crusades
while wondering why
your salary is less than a ditch digger's,
when you tell me
that you will no longer consider yourself
a member of the working class

and that you will feed those innocent minds
less patriotism
and more internationalism,
then you can wish me
"Happy New Year!"

You there, good man of God,
how come you are so far away
from your church and pulpit?
Ah yes, you are showing us
that you're a regular guy
mixing with the publicans and sinners
and even taking a drink with us
because attendance has been poor lately,
when you take seriously the great rebel
whose example you profess to uphold
and stick your own neck out a little
(you won't be nailed to a hunk of wood,
just be investigated by some committee
and maybe lose your job),
tell your flock to give unto Caesar
only what belongs to Caesar
meaning a good kick in the pants,
then you can wish me
"Happy New Year!"

You there, respectable housewife,
your kids at home
with a babysitter riding herd over them,
taking a breather
from your 365-days-a-year occupation
of world's most liberated woman,
so immersed in good holiday spirits
as you kiss every cat at the stroke of twelve,
you don't even kick up a fuss
if somebody cops a feel,
when you tell me

that you will raise your kids
to have an absolute respect for life
be it white, black, red, yellow,
heathen or Christian,
irrespective of which side
of whatever curtain
and that you will disown them
should they ever become soldiers,
munition workers
or take up any other such non-productive
line of endeavor,
then you can wish me
"Happy New Year!"

But go on, all of you,
with your belabored gaiety
and your frantic escapism,
see how long you can run away
from the past 365 days of frustration
hoping that next 365 will be
less frustrating,
the silly rumor that ostriches
hide their heads under the sand
was started by humans
but I wonder what the ostriches say about us?

Sure, I'll have that drink now…!

"1 Mayo, El Dia del Trabajo" (1986), The Permanent Collection of the National Museum of Mexican Art.

IV

WHERE ARE THE VOICES?

Where Are the Voices?

Where are those loud voices
That rang through the land in its towns and cities,
In its hop fields and lumber camps,
In its textile mills and steel mills,
In its wheat fields and its waterfronts,
Voices so loud that entire police forces would attend
 their rallies
To give riot-gun ovations and Billy club caresses?
Where is the voice of the young Swedish hobo
 song writer
Who the mine bosses stood against a prison wall
 in Utah
And filled his body full of bullets
Like his colleague of two thousand years earlier, the
 young Jew hobo carpenter
Who the disgruntled money changers impaled on a cross
 with rusty nails
And two thousand years later are still pounding those
 nails?
Where are the voices of the young Aztec peón
Shouting Land and Liberty
Who the Hacendado and Standard Oil puppets
 silenced forever with an ambush
And the young Spanish poet
Who so infuriated that bosom buddy of the State
Department
That his cutthroats saw to it those hands would write no
 more poetry
While across the Tyrrhenian Sea
A sad-eyed Italian suffered a similar fate?
Where are the voices of the two Italian dreamers
Who in Massachusetts were strapped to a chair by the
 sons of Cotton Mather

And barbecued with high voltage
And the anarchist editor who because he wrote too much
Was found by a bullet on a dark New York Street
While the "finest" just shrugged their shoulders
And the passionate Jewess who fleeing one tyranny
Had found only another tyranny and came back broken?
Where are the voices of the half-Indian Wobbly
Who a committee of solid citizens, using tortures no
　　Indian ever dreamed of
Could not get the satisfaction of hearing one cry of pain
Or plea for mercy from his lips
And a fellow worker of his, not quite so stoic,
Castrated and hung by his toes from a railroad trestle
Shouting, "Kill me, you bastards!"
And the burly miner who jumped bail to go to the
　　Workers' paradise
And lushed up his last years in disappointment?
Where are the voices of the stout-hearted Haymarket
　　Germans
Who in Chicago had started a tide
No army of pinkertons and finkertons could hold back
And paid with their lives to bring
The extra hours of leisure time
That working fools like you and me now enjoy?
Where are those voices?
Have they been buried beneath labor-management
　　contracts,
Buried beneath closed-shop agreements and no-strike
　　clauses,
Buried beneath banquets for pie-cards and their shop
　　owner buddies
With patriotic posters showing labor shaking hands with
　　management
Under the gaze of a beaming Uncle Sam,
Buried ever so deeply beneath overtime paychecks?

Have the voices been drowned out by technicolor
soundtracks,
Radio and television,
Juke boxes and squeaky muzaks,
Long voluptuous high-powered automobiles
And bright new vacuum cleaners
All through the miracle of easy-term time payments
Insipidly singing to us,
"Where else but here could you have it so good?"
Have those voices been outshouted by the voices of the
cynic
And the tired radical
And the objective analyzer
Loudly insisting the movement is dead?
The old timers are gone, but their voices they never took
with them,
Their lingering voices blending in
With an ever-growing symphony,
Bursting out from the Earth's four corners
From Caribbean jungles and North African deserts
To Arizona reservations and South African slum towns,
From sunny Mediterranean islands and Catalonian alleys
To Kilimanjaro foothills and sunny Southland lunch counters,
Heard above the tanks and guns in Budapest streets
And heard above banana-bought airplanes
Roaring low over Central American rooftops,
Heard in the defiant anthems of Bantu men and women
Falling beneath apartheid clubs and bullets,
Laughing along with walking commuters
Who are hitting Jim-Crowed bus lines
Real hard in the pocketbook
And such voices can be heard
By all but the very deaf!

From Northern Minnesota's scrub-timbered wastes
To Southern Arizona's dry hillsides
And from Puget Sound's bleak islands
To central Missouri's padded cells
Still echo the voices of the
Conscientious young men
Who are proud they did not pay taxes
The year atomic power was brought into this World.
From a Sun-drenched Southwestern mesa
A proud people living a life of values so ancient
Yet so new to invading barbarians
Who seek to destroy that which they cannot understand
To a group of would-be mariners
Attempting to sail a ship into nuclear waters
And gaining the love of a people
Whose fishermen die fishing for contaminated sea food.
From missile bases in Nebraska and Wyoming
Where youths picket around
The clock and suffer broken legs
To a grimy Southern prison cell
Where languishes a small gentle-faced man
Who dares to dream of freedom for his island;
Down the long broad highways
With a bushy-haired anarchist Catholic
Spreading his own gospel of revolution
To a dingy second-floor office
On the dingy street
Of one of the dingiest metropolises
Spreading a badly needed message
And the roll call goes on.
Those are the voices of men and women
Who seek no refuge in gray-flannel-suited anonymity
Or khaki-colored respectability
Or chromium-plated mediocrity.

Those are the voices of the inheritors
Of a million years' struggle
From primeval quadruped to quixotic biped
And neither Roman arena
Nor medieval floggings,
Inquisitional torture chambers,
Guillotines,
Firing squads,
Electric chairs
Nor congressional investigations
Can still those voices
For those are the voices only Freedom can silence!

"Lucía González de Parsons," (1986), The Permanent Collection of the National Museum of Mexican Art.

Youngstown Revisited

The waters of the Mahoning
are no longer hidden,
the Jungle of steel mills
is being deforested
but the rust remains.

The unionized steel workers
who expected their children
to carry on the struggle
must now watch them
fling burgers for peanuts.

The steel mill owners
have gone to greener pastures;
from the Valley of Mahoning
they took all their gold
but left behind the rust!

Third Shift

You with your million
        evil green window
        eyes,
You swallow me every
        evening,
And puke me every
        morning.
Damn you!

"Ben Fletcher," (1986), The Permanent Collection of the National Museum of Mexican Art.

Depot Park Night Blues

Lonesome depot lights
Caressing the park's night leaves.
A solitary water fountain singing an aria
With a few philharmonic crickets
In an angry hot breeze.
Pinch-hitting for the moon
Hidden behind a night hot cloud
The depot clock shines
His flat dull face
On the bowed heads of
The benches' nocturnal inhabitants
Who have nowhere else to go,
In the train-whistle night's
Angry hot breeze.

"United Miners" (1988), The Permanent Collection of the National Museum of Mexican Art.

Clinchfield Mine Disaster

On the seventeenth of October
in the year of Nineteen-Sixty-Five,
deep in a coal mine in West Virginia
Andy Kuruscz spent his last day alive.
Like most miners in the hilly mine
country of West Virginia
here the roads never run straight,
Andy Kuruscz had himself a family
As did the most of his six fellow workers
who were in the mine with him
that Sunday morning.
Anyone who did not have a wife and kids
would more than likely be footloose and fancy free
going to some show, visiting some girlfriend,
sleeping off a Sunday morning hangover
or just sleeping late because it was Sunday morning
but certainly not spending a week-end deep down
in the bowels of Mine Number 2.
When Andy kissed Mary Lou the night before
and waved at his three kids as he left for work,
and when Bob Savage said to Pearl, "See you tomorrow"
as he walked out the door,
and when Ike Moats gave Melinda a fond pat
and tousled the hair
of his four kids as he picked up his lunch bucket,
and Ken Kerr gave Flossie a hug
while thinking fondly of their grown kids
as he put on his cap,

and Carl Banish waving goodbye to his Pearlie,
his old Mother and ten kids as he stepped out the door,
and young Charley Lantz giving his young wife
one more lingering kiss while looking fondly
at his sleeping child
before going to his car,
and Clell Leedy on his way down
the rambling hill-country road,
Sunday would be just another goddam day
grubbing for coal deep in the guts
of Mine Number 2.
Deep down in the mine
where there was no sun, sky or cloud,
a layer of coal dust
was for Andy Kuruscz a last shroud.
Andy and his six fellow miners
had given up their week-end
to do some maintenance work
so full production could be had
for the week ahead.
The automated mining machine that was being used
struck an overhead power-line
sending sparks flying in all directions
and short-circuiting the power,
but soon there was more light
than was bargained for or wanted.
For the miners who were spending their final week-end
deep in the intestines
of Mine Number 2.
Deep down in the mine
no pillows for their heads
Andy Kuruscz and his co-workers
laid stone-cold dead.

The miners' union sent its representatives to the scene
to see what could be done
but all that could be done was to stand around on top
while the fire raged on in the mine down below.
The representatives from the miners' welfare
and retirement fund
in their statement to the press
said that disaster and funeral benefits
were being arranged for
within twelve hours upon it being determined
that the miners
were dead
and the officials of the mine company breathed
a sigh of relief
that it had not happened during the week
with full-time crew
where scores of men could have perished
leaving scores of widows and children
to receive benefits from a fire that raged
deep in the innards
of Mine Number 2.
Deep, deep down
beneath the West Virginia bush
the hissing of flames
was the requiem for Andy Kuruscz.
The deep intestines
of Mine Number 2
belched through its maw the bodies
of seven more miners
sending them on their way to join
the hosts of miners before them
who have met their final reward
in some bituminous Golgotha.

Down below
far beneath the Appalachian Sun
and the Appalachian sky
and far beneath the Appalachian earth
deep down in the bowels
of Mine Number 2
where the Sun never shines nor
does the Moon and the breezes
never blow
was found a message scrawled in chalk:
"We can't get by it!"
Mary Kuruscz
at the end of the day
dried off her eyes
and put Andy's stuff away.

Un Corrido Borincano

Gang around while I tell you a story
I hope it will cause you some thinkin'
How poverty had caused a young farmer
To sail from his home in Borinquen
The sugar crop did not sustain self and family
And so he fell in with the notion
To find his fortune on the mainland
Where the statue faced out to the ocean.
He was told of many jobs on the mainland
Where they pay fantastic wages
And he could send home some of his paycheck
Each week to his family courageous
To go to a strange land and language
Did not disturb him at all
For in order to be a Puerto Rican
One must have plenty of gall
He took his hat off to no man
His blood no one could erase
Flowing through his valiant arteries
Was the pride of more than one race
From the sun-swept grass of Andalusia
And from the drum-throbbing Gold Coast
With a dash of Arawak maiden
Who'd been there to welcome them both
He had his own way of speaking the language
That gave pain to the academician
Who has never had an inheritance
Of illiteracy plus malnutrition
He kissed his young wife and five children
And graying mother he gave one last embrace
Went down to the ticket office
And booked passage for the promised place
He came to the land of plenty
Found himself room in a tenement

And like the others of his race
A smelly tannery his place of employment
Where he lived was crowded and dirty
The street was foul with neglect
His job was filthy and thankless
Yet each week he mailed home a check
To buy food for his five little children
Medicine for his dear old mother
And pay the doctor bill of his sweet woman
Whose belly was large with another
Till one day the tannery slowed down operations
The orders were coming in slow
The boss said to cut down the
Number of workers
And the Puerto Ricans were the first to go
As the weeks went on things got no better
Even gringos were walking the street
In the barrio people were getting restive
And the cops were putting on the heat
If you ever are born again, brothers
Be sure it's with a fair skin
Be unable to speak with an accent
That's the only way you can be "in"
One night down a dark street he was walking
His feet had gotten a bit sore
He saw a man through a plate glass window
Counting change alone in his store
When he saw that pile of loose money
He thought of his hungering kin
His good sense for the moment had left him
And through the door he slowly walked in
On his way to the proprietor's counter
He picked up a child's baseball bat
Went to where the man was
counting his money
And said, "I'll take all of that"

When the owner saw his grim appearance
For the police he began loudly to yell
So the other in panic did strike him
And with one last grasp for his money, he fell
Falling forward from the blow
That was dealt him
On a sharp corner he struck hard his head
When the police came to investigate later
On the floor they found the store owner dead
Looking for clues was the detective
But he saw his case wouldn't be hard
As the thief was pocketing the money
He had dropped his security card
Next morning at the First National
They apprehended the young Puerto Rican
Who was at the money order window
Sending a check to the folks in Borinquen
"I did not mean to kill anyone" he protested
I only wanted money to send home
To my wife, children and poor old mother
Because in this strange place I'm alone."
"Lone shop-keeper killed by Puerto Rican"
Were the tabloids' broad headlined report
The judge and the jury felt righteous
When the Jibaro made his appearance in court
The case against him was presented most strongly
No one to speak in his defense was there
The jury took five minutes and the judge told him
He was to die in the electric chair.
He was taken to a dark dreary building
Where machine-gun guards manned the approaches
And was assigned his suite in the death house
Amid the smell of death and cockroaches.
In his cell awaiting date of execution
He sat staring at the floor
His eyes saw only the little homestead
He had left a few months before

Till one night his cell door was opened
And to the priest's low mumbling talk
He marched slowly down that dim passage
On that last wearisome walk
They strapped him securely in the hot seat
And put a metal cap on his head
He cried for the last time, "Ave Maria"
Twelve minutes later they pronounced him dead
In a suburban home the judge was entertaining
His friends with a vintage of imported make
While uptown a well-fed prosperous landlord
Sat down to his beer and porterhouse steak
Fly away, fly away little dove bird
Fly away to your blue Caribbean
Tell the little family of their young farmer
Who'll never come back to Borinquen.

Appalachian Thanksgiving

The winds whistle through the valleys
past the deserted mines
through the cracks in the tarpaper shack
past the newsprint wallpaper
where on a bare wooden table
along with the hog jowls and hominy grits
is a letter from Cousin Bob in Chicago
who is living on welfare checks
asking to please send a picture
of the mountains.

3 AM Blues

The windows of
    The watchman's shanty
        Fogging up,
Who the hell,
Hung that damn nude
On the wall?

The Man with the Nightstick

(With apologies to Edwin Markham)

Bowed with the weight of corruption he leans
Upon his nightstick and glares all around,
The emptiness of thought on his face,
And on his back the cans of mace.
What made dead to rapture and despair,
A thing that neither grieves nor hopes,
Receptive only to clout, a brother to the ox?
Whose were the hands that slanted this brow?
Whose breath blew out the light
Where his brains should be?
Is this the thing that was made and gave
To have dominion over our homes and streets;
To protect our old and young;
To see that they, along with us, are safe?
Is this the shape that a man was meant for?
There is no shape more terrible than those,
More deaf to the cries against the World's greed,
More blind to the signs and portents of the soul,
More packed with danger to the universe.
What gulfs between him and the seraphim!
Slave of an inadequate ego, what to him
Are dreams of liberty and the freedom of speech?
What knows he of the pleasure of song,
The freshness of dawn in the reddening of his nose?
Through this dread shape betraying,
Plundering, profaning and disinheriting,
Underling of the powers that rule this World
Blind to protests and prophecy.
o masters, lords, and rulers of all lands,
Is this your handiwork you gave to man,
This monstrous thing distorted and soul-quenched?
How is it possible to straighten up this shape

Touch it again with humanity;
Make him look upward and see the light;
Open his mind to music and dreams;
Erase once and for all his immemorial infamies
And his immedicable perfidies?
o' masters, lords, and rulers of all lands,
How will the future reckon with
The creators of this thing?
How will his brute answers meet
The questions in that hour,
When the whirlwinds of rebellion shake all shores?
How will it be with kingdoms and kings
With those who shaped him to the thing he is
When this dumb terror can no longer serve his creators
After the silence of centuries?

"Viva La Huelga" (1993), The Permanent Collection of the National Museum of Mexican Art.

Tragedia de Alonso

From Spain where sixty years ago
he first saw the light of day,
he came to this land as a young man
to settle in this town to become a construction worker
and before long he became one of the best tunnel-
workers in the town.

To be a tunnel worker you have to be damn good.
to hunch up twenty feet and more below the surface
chipping away at hard packed clay with a short-handled shovel
is no job for a pantywaist
And Alonso was a damn good "miner."

When you flush your toilet and it works in good order
banishing forever that part of your problems
so that it can flow on to its proper destination,
You have men like Alonso to thank.
he used to ask me over a glass of beer,
"Compañero, why do you fool
around on top with your pick and shovel
Cuando pueden ganar más pá' abajo.

I told him I didn't like dirt hanging over my head!
Yesterday I heard the sad news.
he was working on an open cut
and the shoring planks were a little too far apart.
No doubt the contractor was saving on materials.
you folks who point with pride at your efficient sewer systems,
give a thought to men like Alonso
who worked hard all his life,
and got paid off with a two-ton cave in!

Outa Work Blues

Well, it's a long time on the street
And the rockin' chair money's all gone
It's a long time on the street
And the rockin' chair money's all gone
I'm down to rolling my own
And pickin' butts off the lawn

Went to the employment office
To see what I could find.
I went to the employment office
To see what I could find.
Six hundred other people there
Same thing on their mind.

Told the interviewer
I'd do anything but shovel crap.
I told the interviewer
I'd do anything but shovel crap.
He told me he was sorry
There was only one opening for that.

When I was drawing compensation
They'd hang any job on my neck.
Yes, when I was drawing compensation
They'd hang any job on my neck.
But now that old rockin' chair's busted
They won't let me past the first deck.

President said on television
That things was mighty fine.
The president said on television
That things were mighty fine.
Man at the supermarket tells me
No groceries sold on time.

Suburban Gal

There she stood in the chill November afternoon
with the wind whipping at her bare ankles
among the small group of people gathered
by the tomb of the Haymarket Martyrs
listening as the impromptu orator
told our side of the story.

Later on, as we were sitting in the restaurant
she listened some more as I told of other martyrs
and how today FBI stooges' snap pictures
of everyone who walks into a radical meeting
and I could see that she understood
our side of the story.

Requiem for a Swede

A cold November morn
standing alone against a stone wall
beneath a blue Ute sky

A song writing
accordion playing
itinerant
ballad singing
freedom loving
Son of Man:

                    Haegglund,
                    Hillstrom,
                    Hill

Far from his boyhood Gaevle
where his first years were known
across a continent
and
across an ocean
in the land of Viking grand sires
where the sun first warmed his face.

The same Sun looks down
on capitalist rifles
whose targets are usually Men of Toil
                    Men of Vision
                    and Men of Agitation.

A Mormon voice barks out:
                    Fire!!!
A group of rifles bark out:
                    Bang!!!

Somewhere in a deep green forest
weighted with the ravages of centuries
a stately pine crashes to the ground.

Over the prison yard's black cinders
spreads another hue
the color of the working- class standard
and the sun warms that face
for the last time.

Somewhere
lodged in a decaying log
a small pine cone sends forth
a green shoot.

Somewhere
in a Rebel Valhalla
playing an accordion
singing a song
a spirit waits
for a class conscious
Armageddon.

"Joe Hill," (ca, 1980s), The Permanent Collection
of the National Museum of Mexican Art.

Requiem for 'Two Dago Reds'

Tu, Nicola,
Non set morto,
Et tu Bartolo,
Non sei morto,

Just because they didn't like your ideas
They hung a rap on you,
These good upright people
Of the Commonwealth of Massachusetts.
They tried to tell the World
That you the fish peddler
And you the shoe cobbler
Pulled a heist,

Ma chi era i brigandi?

They pulled every dirty trick in the book,
These upright citizens.
They really stacked the cards
Against you two
Who only wanted to sell fish
And make shoes
And tell your fellow workingmen
Of a better world.

The best legal minds in the country
Showed where they were wrong
But the judge kept a deaf ear.
The Portygee hood who was in the pokey
With you two
Who said he didn't care for guinea radicals
Saw your families come to visit you
And the little kids who wondered
When their Daddy would come out

And play with them again,
Broke down and told the cops
And told the lawyers
How you two couldn't have pulled the heist
But the Judge wouldn't listen.

Questa vecchio scorpone Thayer,

He hated foreigners, especially radical ones
And by the living god of Massachusetts
And all that was holy
He was going to see you two burn.
That's what he boasted as he was playing golf
While you the fish peddler
And you the shoe cobbler
Were sitting in prison
Away from your families
And away from the children
And away from the fellow workingmen
Whom you loved so well.

No Nicola, non sei morto
E tu Bartolo, non sei morto
Ma quant' genti ricordan' il vecchio Thayer?

They had their way,
These scions of the witch burners
And betrayers of the Indians
Who saved them from starvation,
These sons of Cotton Mather.
They shaved your heads
And strapped you in the chair.
They placed the metal plates on your heads
And the bands on your limbs
And turned on the voltage
And watched you burn!

Chi era i brigandi?
Chi era i scorponi!

These men who adjusted the bands,
Who threw the switch,
Who took you from your homes and people
And from the World.
This old man
Who in the name of the Commonwealth of
Massachusetts
Pounded that gavel for the last time.
How many remember their names?
But you, fish peddler
And you, shoe cobbler
The World will not forget you,

Nostri Fratelli,
Nuestros Hermanos,
Unsere Brüder,
Adelfia Mas.

Whatever languages, wherever workingmen
Who dream of a better World come together
Your names live on in their hearts.

No Nicola,
No Bartolo,
Questo e certo,
Non sei morto!

"Justicia Para Los Campesinos," (1979) The Permanent Collection of the National Museum of Mexican Art.

A Difference

The scissor-bill who spits
        at my placard,
Hurls obscenities
And yells,
        "Go back to
Russia!"
        Him I do not feel
too angry at;
        He only has a long
way to go.
But the person who glances
        around furtively
Before confidentially whispering
        to me,
                "I agree with you;
What you're doing is great!"
                That one I cannot
        stand;
That one, he is going
nowhere!

City Central Blues

With a window of iron
and a mattress of wood,
a concrete floor
where many a rounder
has stood.

Contemplating
the small horizon
with a bit of despair,
pensively seated
on a porcelain chair.

Sucking a cigarette
then flicking the air,
each ash
belonging to the past
burning away like life itself
the years stacking
like books on a shelf.

Thoughts before
never understood
till face to face
with a window of iron
and a mattress of wood.

Two December Songs For 1982

I.
Snaking around the block
from the Unemployment Compensation
Office
the early morning waiting line
of new applicants
look at the Christmas decorations
on the businesses across the street
while telling the canvasser from
voter registration to go to hell,
as Booger King's Stars and Stripes
are whipped into further ragged tatters
by the cold December wind.

II.
Praise SOMEBODY for
little blessings!

Here
they do a better job
of calling out surnames
than down at
Immigration Service!

"Two December Songs for 1982" (1992), Scratchboard, From: *de Kansas a Califas & Back to Chicago: Poems and Art*, MARCH/Abrazo Press, 1992. P. 42-43.

Speranz!

A small green leaf
Breaks its way
Thru a crack in the pavement,
Glories briefly
In its new-found freedom,
Then withers;
But the root beneath
Grows
Stronger and stronger.

"Quo Vadisimus?" (1992), Scratchboard, From: *de Kansas a Califas & Back to Chicago: Poems and Art*, MARCH Abrazo Press, 1992. P13.

V

DE KANSAS A CALIFAS & BACK TO CHICAGO

Peregrinaje en Hannibal, Missouri

En el jardincito
de la casa
de Mark Twain,
lugar de niñez y juventud
de un gran escritor,
encuentro orto carnal,
un pimpollito de verdolagas

Elk City Night Stop

The barreling semi-trucks,
The autos,
The sprawling suburbia of motels
With air-conditioned closed-circuit TV;

I hear the thunder of hoofbeats:
The Buffalo are coming back!

Laguna

After exasperating miles
Of tourist-trap freeway-avenues
The sight of a cluster of adobe houses
On a hillside
Blending with the terra cotta
Landscape,
A harmony that is not even disturbed
By the contrast of a whitewashed
Spanish mission
Is a melodious but firm reminder
That people were born
To blend with the Earth.

Quo Vadisimus?[1]

The West ain't what it used to be,
And it's getting ain'tier every day;
All those small bus stop towns
That had a special place en mi corazón,[2]
(Never mind the long history of hassle
Contra Raza y Indigena[3])
Have become obscene imitations
Of Las Nalgas[4] and Miami Bitch;
Swimming pool and closed-circuit TV motels,
Colonel Sandhog and MacDunghills,
With authentically expensive
Indian curio shops,
(Mientras los indios fueron desempleados[5]
So damn long they can't afford to
Emborrachar[6] anymore) y los
Fancy cafés and clubs strung along the freeways
All after the bucks of the bored suburbanites
And I can't find a sack of Bull Durham
Anywhere!

1 where are we going?
2 heart, core
3 against the race (Mexicans) and the indigenous
4 (Las Vegas) the buttocks
5 meanwhile, the Indians have been unemployed
6 get drunk

Puridád

And then comes the Desert,
The pure clean Desert,
That great fullness
That reminds the frantic motorists
Of their own EMPTINESS

Mojave Desert, 1982

Yosemite, 1982

The bark houses,
The stone mortars,
A complete village
Just like the old days;
All for the tourists!

But the entrances to the
Ceremonial house
And the Sweat Lodge
Are closed off!
They are still in use!

Wa chi taw!
It is good!

Yosemite Night Scene

In the high Sierras
Night comes quickly;
The tall Pines
And the
Taller Mountains
Sing to me:

Solitude can be
The greatest company!

Night on Highway# 1

The dark sky
and the dark Ocean
Shine brightly
around
the even darker
Mountain;

Que poderosas
son las montañas!

Another rainy day
        in San Francisco;
My warmth
        is far away!

Soledad, Califas

Soledad quiere decir,
Solitude en inglés
Pero no hay ningún loneliness
En este pueblito
Off the main highway
En Califas.

En "El Zacatecano"
Onde comí mis huevos con chorizo
While looking at
And listening to the mariachis
On the TV from Salinas
And looking at the Ventana Mountains
Through the front window,
Hay mas pica que el chile.

Out on the distant highway
The Twentieth Century speeds on
To its ultimate oblivion
Pero aqui hay Raza
Por todos lados.

Never mind the history books,
Dice la Palomita,
We never lost Califas!

Mojave, Califas

In the roadside café
A stuffed Mountain Lion stands
With a hand-lettered card,
"Thank you for not touching!"
Pero, Hermanito,
You have already been touched!

How long must such
Indignity continue?

Spirit of the Mountain Cat:
May your Grandchildren
Teach your assassins
The proper path!

Pomona

Like a morning ghost
The snow-capped
Gabrieles
Loom above
The palm trees and
Cottages and motels
And smog
Of the car-culture
Streets
Ever reminding
That eternity
Is NOW!

Never mind;
High above
The smog
The Mountains
Are still
THERE!

Club El Mercado

Cuando moriré
No me importa
Si San Pedro
Me dice
"Vete pa'l otro piso, ese"
Si hay Mariachis allá.
Y si no hay ...
Si todos serán a la Gloria;

No seré el primer indocumentado
Que pasar pá
Las Pearly Gates.

Centinela

Beneath the high street lamp
In the overnight
Trailer Park;
With the encouragement
From the Desert Moon;
The young Saguaro
Maintains his unapproachable
Dignity.

Gabacha Encantada

The Amtrak winds its way through West Texas
Through what the Blue Eyes call "Wasteland"
Puro mesquite, blue sage y nopaltzines
Con zopilotes circling the blue skies above.
Those blue ridges in the distance
Are unoccupied Mexico.
Over the PA system a Texas cracker voice
Is making like a chingon chicharrón
As it proudly lists the Texas features
And historical spots.
West of the Pecos, the millennia
Have cut through the solid rock

Tumbleweeds

When the Tumbleweed
Has finished his days of existence,
The roots that bind him down
To the Earth Mother
Give way
And he can go wherever
The Winds take him.

How much better
Than a tombstone
And the Pearly Gates!

Tumbleweeds #2

Tumbleweeds
Dancing along the Texas highway.
Only flatlands and wheat fields ahead!

Ontá mis adoradas Montañas?
No more Saguaro, también.

¡Solo tus brazos
¡Me pudieron consolar!

"Para Marianna" (1992), Scratchboard, From: *de Kansas a Califas & Back to Chicago: Poems and Art*, MARCH Abrazo Press, 1992. p3

VI

EMPTY HOUSE BLUES

Dos Madrugaditas Two Early Mornings

1) This Morning

On the pillow
There was a book
Where your head
Should have
Been.

2) Sin tu presencia

En este jacal
Tambien las Cucarachas
Me abandonaron.

Without your presence
In this humble hut,
Even the roaches
Have abandoned me.

Prelude to the Moment of Truth

Standing by the mirror
combing her hair
even though the lights are out
and the mirror
reflects nothing
she still combs her hair.
A cool summer breeze that flows
through the open window
is all the covering she has
as she glances over her shoulder
at me
smiling her funny little smile

How La Guitarra Was Born

Long ago, there was a vaquero
who rode alone on the plains
except for his horse,
and his herd of cattle.
He was hungry for a woman,
but there was no woman
for hundreds of miles.
While riding he saw a tree
and chopped it down.
When he peeled the bark off
he saw the wood was a rich golden brown.
With his machete,
he carved the trunk into the form of a woman.
By the campfire at night,
he held the woman of wood on his lap.
With his left hand
he caressed her neck.
With his right hand
he played with her breasts and tummy.
The woman of wood moaned with pleasure
and began to sing.
With happiness in his heart, the vaquero sang along with her.
Each night by the light of the campfire
they sang, and that is how la guitarra was born.

Empty House Blues

Dos meses seems like a long-ass time;
Too damn long hearing one's own heartbeat and
Too damn long feeling no one's flesh but one's own;
Yo sé que los izkuintlis[1] keep me company
But they lack that certain algo.

Don't jump to conclusions I still know how to live
Porque la vida vale everything.
Como este fin de semana con la fiesta en el barrio,
I enjoyed myself con todo dar up to the last moment.
All I came to do was already done.

I was ready to go home to feed and walk los izkuintlis,
But my friends told me, "*Agarrale unos taquitos y*
hechale unas cervecitas." ¿Y porque no?
los izkuintlis have become muy philosophical
de comer y cuitlatl[2] tarde en los weekends.

And why should I be in a hurry to go back
To an empty house? Pero aquellos mariachis;
Con sus cuerdas y sus pinches trompetas,
They take the empty house and
Put it right inside of my shirt.

1 dogs in Nahuatl
2 excrement in Nahuatl

7 Springtime Haiku

after the civil defense siren
      yes
even the crows sound beautiful

——

the forlorn little icicle
      loosing hold
becomes its own teardrop

——

last snow on the ground
in the traffic humming
      twilight
      the first frog

——

wise little pigeons
they know
      how to decorate
the courthouse

——

rising from
    the dead leaves
green resurrection
the pine tree
    having stood solitary
now has company

—

the snow is gone
    once again, the old creek
        is lined with mud, grass
            & kids

Macuilhaicuh

(Cinco Haiku Chicanos)

Ya vamos a comer elotes,
Tocan huapango
Los grillos.

—

¡Oralé chapulín
Cántame más
¡Y deja mi lechuga!

—

Rojo como los labios
De mi chata,
Y son los chiles.

—

Como pechos de jovencitas,
Los frijoles en sus vainas.

—

Cantan alegre las ranas,
Ya el verano es barbudo.

"La Lucha Continua" (ca, 1970s) The Permanent Collection of the National Museum of Mexican Art.

VII

WE ARE STILL AROUND

Poema por El Dia de la Raza

Muchos siglos antes los Chinos[1]
came to these shores
And saw that they were not
the first people that came here.
For many Moons they sailed along
the Pacific Coast
Taking notes for their history books,
swapping semillas, cuentos y palabras[2]
Before sailing back to China.

Some centuries later some Scandinavians
came across the other Ocean,
Real rough batos who were accustomed
to coming on pretty tough
But when they found out that those whom
they called the Skraelings
Could be every bit as rough, they sailed back
To their fjords and flaxen-haired rucas.[3]

It has been rumored that some Celtics
also sailed over
and must have liked what they saw
Because it has further been rumored that they
stayed around and became
Light-skinned Indians because it is rumored
That they never bothered to go back to Wales.

All of the early navigators knew, be they
güero[4] Vikings, prieto[5] Polynesians
o quien sabe quién,[6]

That when Mountains disappear
beneath one horizon
or rise up from another horizon,
This Earth of ours cannot be flat;
So never mind what the school teachers
try to tell you,
Este cabrón,
Cristobal Colón,
Cristóforo Colombo,
Christopher Columbus,
Whatever your particular ethnocentric bias
chooses to call him,
He did not think of anything new.

Si el Rey y la Reina de España really believed
This Earth of ours was as flat as a tortilla,
They wouldn't have given old Chris
any second thoughts,
Pero con sus corazones de ladrones[8]
they recognized in this fregón
Immense possibilities of empire
or they would have never
Invested any of their parasitic wealth
in his grandiose idea.

Pero aquél Cristobal, his reputation as a
sea captain was so notorious that
The only way he would have any crew at all
Was for their majesties to man his three ships
with "volunteers" from the
Spanish prisons and the invasion
was soon under way.

Since that day that old Chris landed on these shores
and thought he was meeting the sons of Krishna,
Some sinvergüenza[7] with a badly-misplaced
sense of humor
Has designated for posterity "
as "El Dia. de la Raza,"
Pero guachale, even Raza cannot remember
when Raza first came to these shores
And even if some of us have become mezclados con
Español, portugués, africano, francés o Anglo-Sajón,
one thing we know fo' shu'
La Raza did not begin in 1492!

Their historians refer to us as primitive, backward
and historically unprogressive,
Pero nuestro maiz, papas, gitomates, calabazas,
tabaco,
chocolate, camotes, vainilla, chiles y cacahuates,
Saved their so-called "Old World" from certain
Starvation and probable revolution;
Helped them to feed their hungry armies and navies
so they could be progressive enough
to colonize the World.

Yes, it can be said that we backward and
historically unprogressive descamisados
Have done our part towards bringing into being
capitalism and the "modem age,"
Though we would much prefer to be
remembered for jamacas, toboggans y elotes.

Pero para nosotros, "El Dia de la Raza"
todavía no lo llegue;
It is still somewhere in the future.
In spite of cannon balls, Gatling guns, bullets,
missionaries, rot-gut whisky,
typhoid and small pox-infested blankets,
scalpel-happy abortionists and the
bad arithmetic of the census takers,
We are still around and we intend to stick around
for quite a while longer
and for a damn good reason;
You see, we were practicing ecology and
the classless society for
thousands of years before
Our "civilizers" even had words for these things!

Ixtachilatlan aik ixpolihuiz!

1 many centuries before the Chinese
2 seeds, stories and words
3 gals
4 blond
5 dark, swarthy
6 or who knows who
7 shameless
8 thieves

This is The Land

On the Sun swept llanos
Where imperceptible chants of long-dead tribesmen
And imperceptible hoof beats of long-dead buffalo
Are lost on the ears of the speeding motorist
And barreling semi driver.

The Sun beats down upon the parched grass
And naked rock outcroppings
Of the horizon-less eternity of flatlands.

Flatlands of the Dakota, the Arapaho, the Kansa, the Kiowa
And the escaped ante-bellum fugitive slave
And the sod busting homesteader
And the farmed-out Okies and Arkies
Y los braceros y los alambres y los mojados.

Where millenniums before la Raza
Rested on their long trek from the Bering Straits
To Anahuac, Tenochtitlan y Mayab
Y dos mil generaciones despues
Are returning to their old tramping grounds.

Great endless sea of no water where a silent Jack Rabbit
Can be mistaken for a scrub tree
And where a scrub tree can be mistaken for a prairie dog
By the speeding motorist and barreling truck driver
Out in the distance-less infinity of unbroken sitting-duck sky
Where loneliness can be measured according to how much gas
Is left in the tank and how far it is to the next town
Where Goodyear four-plies rolling over asphalt and concrete
Tamp down the Western Earth that was once tamped down
By herds of buffalo stretching from horizon to horizon

Only to be slaughtered en masse by the invader
To starve the original plainsmen into submission
When Gatling guns, rotgut whiskey, and typhoid infected blankets
Were not doing the job fast enough

And now the invader's grandsons press their speedometers
To get away from all this endlessness
And the Sun makes its exit from the western edge of the sky
When the land becomes an ocean of flame
Burning away into the flat mighty cinder
That emerges with an ashy pale glow
When the pallid flapjack tortilla moon
Comes out to pinch-hit for the Sun

And the flapjack tortilla moon is momentarily eclipsed
By an airliner with its human cargo
Of dozing night-reading passengers
To whom the Great Plaines is something vaguely remembered
From grammar school geography books
As they idly contemplate Disneyland and North Beach.

And somewhere

A coyote

Howls.

Tenochtitlán

It has been so long that I have not seen you
so long that I have not walked your streets
so long that I have not been intoxicated by your altitude.
Tenochtitlán,
Queen of cities,
Survivor of volcanoes, earthquakes, pestilences, invasions
and your millenniums;
Tenochtitlán,
the last time I saw you
the volcanoes could be seen from deep within your streets,
but now I am told that is no longer possible,
the Mountains can no longer be seen!

Beneath your starlit night sky
in Garibaldi Plaza where your mariachis
gnawed away at my heart with your music and songs,
I am now told the stars no longer shine.
Don't tell me that Chicago's air is cleaner than yours!

Tenochtitlán,
Virgin streetwalker of my soul,
where your tequila, your mescal, your cerveza, your pulque
along with your goddamn seven thousand feet
grinds my brains into sausage and cook my legs into macaroni,
I want to see you again!

I want to walk again in your streets and your markets and your parks;
I want to see again your museums and your galleries
that bear testimony to the wealth and immensity
of the history and culture of our raza!

I want to see your street vendors who will hustle anything
from fried cactus worms to lottery tickets.
I am not afraid of your twenty million inhabitants;
I want to see them too,
But, also...
I want to see the stars,
And...
I want to see the Mountains!

Enganadora

You call yourself Latina
And you tell everyone,
"Qué hay nada más' que la
Sangre de los Conquistadores,"
Flowing through your veins.
Pues, yo sé que...
There's no status
In being a conquistador,
Pero digame, Chiquita,
If your blood comes from
The sunny Mediterranean,
Por qué no tienes nalgas redondas,
And what's that blue spot
Doing in between them?

"Ricardo Flores Magon" (1990), The Permanent Collection of the National Museum of Mexican Art.

Integrity

"As long as the grass shall grow"
So said the old treaties
And it must be so
For the grass has stopped growing
For the Red Man.
But the grass still grows
For the white man.
In his parks
And lawns
Green and beautiful
Watered daily from reservoirs
Now covering the tribal land.

Reservation Xmas

On the reservation
The sleigh and reindeer
Never come.
For the little Indian kids
Santa is the man
With eyes set close
In a florid face
Wearing a steel helmet
And a flag on his shirt.
On his charging
Bulldozer
He chases the little
Indian kids
From their homes in the woods
Seeing to it they join
The kids of other minorities
In the big city slums.

Brings the Pipe

He grew up on the Plains
The Plains that his Fathers before him
Had defended against alien marauders
And from his Fathers he knew well
The pride and sorrow of his nation's history
So to him the white man's battles were
Of little concern.
When he failed to report for his army induction
The feds wasted little time
They hauled him off of the reservation
To appear before a federal judge
And as happened to many others in those years
Who did not choose to heed the call of their peers
He was sentenced to a Federal Correctional
Institution.
When he passed through those gates
Like all new "fish" who were in quarantine
He had to undergo the psychiatric interview
And the bug doctor who for a screw
Wasn't really mean
Just a talkative patriotic sort
That didn't seem to dig conscientious objection
Liked to read the riot act
To those sent up on selective service violation.
He would come on with the usual jive
About misguided revolt against parental authority
Neglecting one's duty to flag and country

And for Brings The Pipe he added a special pitch.
He wanted to know why of all people
An original American
The son of a warrior nation
Did not want to take part
In his country's valorous crusade for liberation.
"Hah! My country," snorted Brings The Pipe,
"I am 22 and cannot buy one glass of whiskey!"
And then with his own sly smile
He suggested to the doctor,
"I will make a deal with you,
You guys keep the treaty that you made with
My Grandfather,
I will fight in your battles for you!"
It was then the usually loquacious prison doctor
Found it convenient to bring this interview
To its conclusion.

The Sun Believer

My father told me the story of a town where he lived as a young man and how one time there was a very big trial to which people came from many miles around.

This trial dragged on for many days, for the freedom of more than one was at stake.

It looked rather hopeless until the defense lawyer found an old man who was to be the key witness.

He was an Indian, one who had never taken the white man's religion, and so he continued to believe as his Nation did in the days before the white men came to disturb their peace.

The lawyer for the prosecution objected to this witness since he did not believe in the white man's god, he would be unable to take the oath on the white man's bible, therefore any testimony this witness would give would be subject to doubt.

The judge, too, had his doubts but he said, "Wait!" and he called the old man up to his bench. "Now you understand," he said to the old man, "that here in the white man's courtroom it is necessary to swear by God. Now I understand that instead of worshiping a supreme being as we do, you consider the sun to be your god. How are we to know that we can accept the word of a man that in this day and age still practices a primitive religion?"

The old man looked the judge square in the eye and replied, "Yes, my god is the Sun. The Sun gives us light and warmth and life. Without the Sun, no life in this World would be possible. That, your own scientists will tell you. You cannot prove that your white man's god exists, for you have never seen your god. You only take the word of other men and not the words that come from your heart. When I pray, I pray with my own words and nobody else's and they are words from my heart. You wonder if my belief is binding enough that you can accept my word as truth. Before you many men have sworn on the white man's bible and told lies. For that you punish them. If I were to lie I would punish myself, for if I would lie, my truth from then on would always be suspected."

The judge after hearing the old man's words said he would make his ruling only in the interests of expediency.

That day more than one person lived the rest of his days in freedom because of an old man's primitive belief in the Sun.

The Downfall of the Disease Giver

Long ago before the God of the Blue Eyes
Was known by the Tribe,
The Tribe knew many Gods and Spirits:
Earth Spirit, Water Spirit, Sky Spirit, Corn Spirit,
Buffalo Spirit, Fish Spirit, Moon Princess, and many
  others
Who were believed in and loved by the Tribe.
Only one Spirit was feared, and that was Disease-Giver,
Who terrorized everyone.
Everyone but one crazy young man named Tall Coyote.
Tall Coyote laughed at Disease-Giver
And said he did not believe in him.
So why should he be afraid of him?
The rest of the Tribe shook their heads sadly, for
  they knew
For such defiance, Disease-Giver would punish
Poor crazy Tall Coyote.
Sure enough, one day Disease-Giver accosted
  Tall Coyote
In front of all the Tribe, and said to him:
"Tall Coyote, I have come to kill you!"
That crazy Tall Coyote, he just laughed and said:
"Disease-Giver, I don't believe in you; you cannot
  hurt me!"

Disease-Giver, he got red in the face and told him to die.
But Tall Coyote kept on laughing.
Again Disease-Giver told him to die;
But Tall Coyote kept on laughing.
After long hours Tall Coyote still laughed;
And Disease-Giver said: “Tall Coyote, please die!”
But Tall Coyote kept on laughing.
Disease-Giver said: “Please, Tall Coyote,
At least have a headache! You are making me lose face!”
But Tall Coyote laughed harder than ever.
It was then Disease-Giver decided
To leave the village of the Tribe
With his tail between his legs,
And was never seen again.
The mind can be a jail, but it can also be a mountain.
Ey—Yaa!

Song of a Second-Class Citizen

I whose fathers
Hunted buffalo on the
    plains
And saved the pilgrims
from starvation
Cannot buy a glass of
    beer
In my own country,

And

I whose fathers
Planted the first cornfields
And built pyramids
Cannot cross a border
In my own continent,

And

I whose fathers
Knew the stench of
    slave ships
And with ancestral memories
Created a new music
Cannot sit where I please
In my own World

And

Whenever I open my mouth
I am told to go back
To where I came from

And

I don't have the fare
Nor
The inclination.

Crystal-Gazing the Amber Fluid

Sitting at this bar
Thinking of places
Afar
In my glass of beer
I see
Thru the smoke-filled haze
of this room
Like a crystal vision
looms
A ribbon of cement
Black line down the middle
Perdition bent
Like a galloping snake
On the make
Thru treeless prairies
And bottomless passes
Ever in motion
Over moon-kissed desert
Toward golden California
Grasses
Stopped only
By a big blue ocean,
Man - - -!
Give me the song
If you can
Of a Greyhound motor's
Tirade
Crawling along
Some old ten-mile grade
Where life can be complete
On a bumpy seat
Watching the great USA
And life itself passing
On its way

And all the while
I say to myself each gulp
of beer
is costing me
another mile!

Tonatlancihuatl[1]

Cuando vienes fresca del baño
Con apozonalotl[2] de jabón
Singing tu canción, tzatziliztlando[3]
Down the drain,
Veo tu glorious body
Pixolo[4] con glistening moisture,
Por la ventana,
Acompañada con ehecatl[5] del verano.

Bajo tus chichis nahuallandas[6]
Yan ne-maco hueytletl,[7]
Es la cárcel de mi corazón

Toda la nentlazolli[8] de nuestra Mundo
Temostli[9] al mictlan[10]
Bajo la fuerza de tu ternura,
Mi Tonatlancihuatl.

1 Shining water woman
2 espuma, foam
3 grito, yell
4 sembrado/emplumado, planted/feathered
5 viento, wind
6 This is a combined Nahuatl (Nahualli) and Spanish (andas) meaning an enchantress and to rate someone with high praise. "Llevar a uno en andas."
7 Donde crece un gran incendio, Where a big fire grows
8 bruja/o, shaman enchantress
9 caída bajar, descend come down
10 lugar de los muertos, realm of the dead

"Pareja Campesina," (1987), The Permanent
Collection of the National Museum of Mexican Art.

Carlos Cortéz, Self Portrait, from Carlos Cumpián, *Coyote Sun*, MARCH Abrazo Press, 1990, p. 25.

CARLOS CORTÉZ KOYOKUIKATL: THE MAN & ARTIST[1]

AFTERWORD BY RENÉ ARCEO

1 Editor's note: This excerpt is from an essay based on a series of interviews Arceo conducted with Cortéz on August 26, 1998, February 18 and 24, 1999, and May 13, 1999. We are grateful to Marc Zimmerman who closely worked with the author on the original essay.

Introduction

Carlos Cortéz was born on August 13, 1923, in Milwaukee, Wisconsin the son of a Mexican father, Alfredo Cortéz and a German-American mother, Augusta Ungrecht. Alfredo Cortéz was a militant member of the Industrial Workers of the World (IWW), known also as the "Wobblies"; he was a construction worker; an itinerant delegate for the IWW, a soapbox orator during the 1912 campaign for "Freedom of expression" in San Diego, California; and a singer in seven languages. Augusta Ungrecht was a socialist-pacifist poet born in Racine County, Wisconsin. As a youth Carlos Cortéz was raised in Milwaukee during the 20's and 30's. At age twenty, he already belonged to the Young People's Socialist League, the Socialist Party's youth group. It was his participation in this group that eventually made him realize he was more of an anarchist than a socialist. From this time on he began to define the philosophical beliefs that shaped him as an anarchist which he explains as follows:

> As an anarchist I am against all forms of coercion, repression and discrimination. I believe in absolute freedom. That is, each person has the freedom to do what each one desires as long as they don't interfere with the freedom of others. Freedom also means respect for others as well as the compromise with others.

Almost fifty and an active member of the Industrial Workers of the World (IWW union) when he joined the Movimiento Artístico Chicano (MARCH) in 1973. Cortéz was recognized as one of the oldest Chicano artists in the country—more than a generation older than almost all those identified as Chicano Movement pioneers. In fact, one of the most famous of those pioneers, Co-founder of the Sacramento, California-based Rebel Chicano Art Front or the Royal Chicano Air Force–R.C.A.F. José Montoya, once told Cortéz, "You were a Chicano way before anybody identified himself as a Chicano."[2]

2 Shifra Goldman, "Mexican And Chicano Workers In The Visual Arts," *Dimensions of the Americas*, p. 296. Goldman distinguishes between those artists

It is clear his parents' influences were profound. As the only son, he inherited from his mother an appreciation for poetry, along with pride in being Mexican. From his father he inherited the love and talent for languages, labor activism and love for music. Cortéz had a significant music collection that he started during his years as a record seller, and he continued to collect music as of 1999 when I interviewed him. His collection is composed of Folkloric music from Latin America, Europe and the United States, including the Anglo-Saxon and Black music traditions. The regional mestizo and indigenous music of Mexico is the largest part of his collection. When Cortéz spoke about his father he did so proudly explaining how he looked indigenous, especially Yaqui—one of the 56 indigenous groups located in Mexico's Northwestern region. Cortéz narrates for us how his parents met:

> Soon after the WWI, my father passed through Milwaukee. My mother shared with me how on one occasion when she attended a Socialist Party meeting with a friend they came across an indigenous-looking guy selling the IWW newspaper. Her friend Clara exclaimed to the Indian, "Why are you selling your newspapers out in front of our meeting?" My mother defended him stating that there wasn't anything wrong with him selling his papers, that he had a right to promote his ideology and that, if they believed in theirs, they shouldn't be afraid to compare it with others. To prove her point, she bought a newspaper from him. This action impressed my father to the point where he took a good look at her and started paying her court. Two years later my old man popped the question.

Cortéz was raised speaking German. His father insisted that his mother speak to him in German so that when he was ready for school, he would already know it. His mother agreed to do this given that his father was also fluent in German. Thus, Cortéz' second language was

identifying themselves as Mexican American or Chicano. By that score, as her Chicano artist son Mario Castillo reminded me when I interviewed him on February 17, 1999, the oldest Mexican American artist in Chicago was María Enriquez de Allen who, born in June 1907, came to Chicago in the 1960s and lived into her nineties.

English. Spanish followed, influenced by his father's many Mexican friends who visited often.

In addition, Cortéz heard a lot of spoken Italian since the majority of the family's friends were Italian. Italian proved to be crucial in his life since it originally became the only means of communication between him and his life-long companion Marianna with whom he would later learn his fifth language, Greek.

Cortéz attended a recital by Flamenco dancer José Greco and there met the woman who he would later marry. Greek national Marianna Drogitis had come to visit her brother in Milwaukee in 1957. Cortéz had known Marianna's brother whom he had befriended while working in a record store. The record store specialized in Greek, Mexican and Puerto Rican music, which satisfied the musical interests and needs of the diverse Milwaukee community. After meeting Marianna, Cortéz stayed in touch with her for a period of nine years, communicating by mail in Italian they both knew. Once Cortéz' parents died in 1966, he decided to sell the house he had inherited and visit Marianna in Greece. When he returned, Marianna accompanied him. They had already made plans to live in the States.

Cortéz' adolescent years were spent exposed to diverse languages and cultures. It was common to come across Jewish people, African-Americans, Native-Americans, Italians, Mexicans, etc. in his home. His family frequently visited indigenous groups in Northeastern Wisconsin where they considered his father a brother because of the respect he had for them and his own apparent indigenous features and complexion. His family was frequently invited as special guests to pow-wow celebrations—events that tourists would have to pay to attend. In the Wisconsin Dells area Cortéz' father was considered an Indian, a brother, one of them. Consequently, his family was treated as any other indigenous family there. During his primary school years, when in the presence of his father with the opportunity to observe his father at ease, Cortéz suddenly realized his mestizo father with his indigenous features truly looked Indian. This experience became a revelation to him, as it reinforced his own sense of identity. During this time he began to create proud portraits of indigenous people.

The Struggles and The Effects of War

During WWII, Carlos Cortéz was jailed for two years at the Sandstone Federal Correctional Institution in Minnesota because he was a conscientious objector ("...because I did not believe in killing other human beings...").[3] In 1944, at age twenty, Cortéz received an official draft notice. When he didn't show up at the draft office, the FBI went to his home and arrested him. His uncle had to get a loan against his farm to pay the $2,000 bail so that Cortéz could be free while awaiting trial. His objections to the draft were based on economic and humanitarian reasons which implied he would never shoot at another draftee. Cortéz comments: "Someone questioned me if I was in favor of Hitler to which I responded, if someone can guarantee me a sure shot at him no one would have to draft me. But to shoot at another draftee, never." The years in jail were years well spent since he had the opportunities to contact other objectors (these included Black Muslims and Jehovah's Witnesses) have access to a good library and further develop his drawing skills by utilizing as models images from magazines like *National Geographic.* During the years he spent in detention, he learned Italian with a teacher who, like himself, had opposed being drafted into the army. This teacher taught Italian to those prisoners who were interested in improving or learning the language. Cortéz was able to use the Italian he learned later when he worked mostly with Italians in the construction industry.

After being released from prison in 1945, Cortéz and his father worked in the construction labor force through the Hod Carriers Union. Later he joined the then diminishing IWW organization. During this time Cortéz started to produce cartoon drawings which, through the process of photo engraving, were reproduced as illustrations for the IWW's newspaper. By the beginning of the 1950's, he began to contribute articles, comments and reviews of films and records. Soon after this his own poetry began to get published. He maintained his connection as graphic artist, poet and illustrator with the IWW newspaper for five decades. At the end of 1950's he began to contribute his first

3 Eugene Nelson, introduction to *Crystal-Gazing The Amber Fluid And Other Wobbly Poems,* by Carlos Cortéz (Chicago: Charles H. Kerr Publishing Co., 1997), 6.

linocut images to the paper since the IWW could no longer afford the increasing costs of photomechanical reproduction.

During the decade of the 1950's, McCarthyism, the cold war, the Korean War, the impact of international espionage and the hysteria over the consequences of the atomic bomb were strong influences which contributed to the instability of progressives and unionists in this country.[4] Senator Joe McCarthy, who represented Cortéz' native state, through his "subversives persecution committee," was shown capturing and processing the 'subversives' among the union leaders associated with the IWW militant traditions. For Cortéz, these experiences reaffirmed his convictions to the point where he, instead of backing up, duplicated his efforts and participation during the following decade. The IWW members or Wobblies were active in the areas of economics, art and literature. Cortéz, as a Wobbly, rejected the Communist Party USA, Marxism and the popular fighting front from the 1930's and 40's, because he felt they were limiting the art and culture through a form of censorship.

It is worthwhile to draw some parallels and make some comparisons here between the IWW artists and those artists in México pursuing similar goals. On an organizational level, a similarity between the IWW and the 1940's Popular Graphics Workshop, also known as Taller de Gráfica Popular or TGP,[5] was twofold: the close relationship between the objective and the themes of the artwork produced by both groups and the political activities members became involved with. The difference between the two groups was that the TGP was an organization created by the Lázaro Cárdenas government (President of México from 1934 to 1940) and subsidized by them. Membership was exclusively for printmaking artists. On the contrary, the Wobblies were economically self-sufficient counting as their sole support their membership fees. In their case, artist members represented only a small portion of their total membership. Cortéz always believed in and was affiliated with collectives, from his early years with the IWW, his incursions with MARCH (Movimiento Artístico Chicano) and the Chicago Mural

4 John Pittman Weber, "Carlos Cortéz," in *Bold Images: Carlos Cortéz, Artist And Poet* (Elmhurst: Elmhurst Art Museum, 1998).

5 TGP will be addressed in the following pages.

Group. Cortéz also came to meet some of the TGP members over the 1990s decade.

The adoption of realism as the preferred aesthetic ideology of the TGP did not force it into the narrow confines of photomechanical reproductions of reality. There was experimentation with the meaning of the prints. Through this vehicle artists expressed their humanist, social, political and economic concerns affecting many places of the world. Their graphics dealt with subjects such as opposition to WWII, to the fascism of Mussolini and Franco, to Hitler's Nazi party and ideology. Their art pronounced them against the reach and consequences of nuclear power, and in favor of peace, farm workers, rural cultural workers who contributed to the economic and industrial development and the teachers who shape the future generations of citizens. It lent general support to the efforts and struggles for social justice throughout the world.[6]

1970's -1980's

Cortéz' life in 1970s and 80s was characterized by his activities in the group MARCH, and his poetry, published for years in IWW publications found its way into several journals and books. Independently and through his association with the Chicago Mural group, now known as the Chicago Public Art Group, he became involved in muralist activities. During this period he painted murals, a long-awaited dream, on his own and with other muralists. By then he was known for his artistic and community contributions, being specifically recognized as a muralist, poet, cartoonist, illustrator and, above all, as a printmaker. During the 1980s he began to exhibit his works on a regular basis at alternative spaces, such as Objects Gallery, Galeria Ink Works, Prairie Avenue Gallery, Galeria Kalpulli, Guild Bookstore, Viva Aztlán and Fiesta del Sol community festivals in addition to the events sponsored by MARCH. As a prolific artist, Cortéz always had some new and fresh

6 Francisco Reyes Palma, "Workshop of Popular Graphics During the Times of Cardenas," *Image of México* (Dallas: Dallas Museum of Art, 1987). Exhibition catalogue.

work to exhibit. Among local Chicago artists, the annual showing of his new works related to the Day of the Dead had become an anticipated event. In 1985 Cortéz baptized his printing press as "Gato Negro Press" with which he published the catalog for the touring exhibition entitled Wobbly: *80 years of Rebel Art*.

During the early 1980s, in a formal ceremony lead by the Mexican Nahuatl cultural leader of the Kalpulli Koakalko spiritual teacher Tlakaele, formally bestowed on Cortéz the name Koyokuikatl (Coyote Song in the Aztec language Nahuatl). Cortéz had met Tlakaele through the local prolific muralist Aurelio Díaz. Tlakaele had chosen a name for him, but Cortéz had already chosen a different name which held special significance for him. The name Koyokuikatl or Coyote Song had come to him during his years in prison where he would frequently hear coyotes howling (singing) in the night. To him this symbolized freedom, the embodiment of the freedom he hoped for. Later Cortéz and his wife Marianna opted to celebrate their commitment to one another with an indigenous wedding ceremony presided over by Tlakaele, blessed by the smoke of sacred copal resin, cedar and sage. Marianna had agreed to this ceremony under the condition that, within one year, Cortéz would be baptized and married in Marianna's Greek Orthodox religion to which he agreed. Usually Cortéz didn't use his adopted name to identify his poetry. He does, however, carve directly onto the wood or linoleum plate, his initials CAC (Carlos Alfredo Cortéz), and when he signs his prints, he does so by drawing the outline of a sitting coyote to honor his adopted name.

Cortéz' persona had a strong physical presence and radiated from him as the poet, printmaker, grandfather without grandchildren, cacique, storyteller, educator, agitator, communicator, illustrator, critic, activist and community artist. His artwork and figure always caught my attention since the first time I met him in the early 1980s. Through his presence and physical appearance he projected a sense of peace, tranquility and knowledge as only a grandfather or a mature person could do. Cortéz lacked arrogance, was devoted to his craft and shared with others the best of himself without expecting something in return. His total work was intended to be shared and to support the needy, those who have the fewest opportunities in life. He was someone who not only didn't retreat from his philosophical principles, but who lived what he preached. I can think of two examples which directly relate to these aspects of Cortéz' persona. The first example is how he always offered his works at the same price to all customers whether they were indigent people at the community cultural festivals in Pilsen or wealthy art collectors at New York's Museum of Modern Art. The second example has to do with his conscious decision to create original multiple prints which could reach broader audiences instead of creating unique, one of a kind works of art such as paintings or sculpture. In this way his prints were available at a lower cost to a larger number of people. When we observe his work, it becomes evident his priority was not to produce a highly and technically processed print—something pretty, or a commercially attractive product. He did not even concern himself with utilizing acid-free paper, which can extend the life of a print for generations; rather his priority is to duplicate and massively reproduce his images and messages. In a way, the fact that he produced prints is clearly not an end for him but was, instead, how he reproduced his messages. Prints are more than merely a practical aspect of his life's work where the technique used is irrelevant as far as the art works' function and content. Thus we can deduce that the priority is the image and the inherent message combined with the natural and artistic touch Cortéz imbeds in his works.

To respond artistically to his world, Cortéz determined to be up to date on the news and events happening around him, especially those affecting, directly or indirectly, matters related to workers, farmers, and Chicanos-Mexicans. The latter was the community to which he devoted much time and effort through his social, labor and political activities. His information sources were not the traditional mainstream commercialized sources which owed themselves to the interests of a consumerist society. He depended on alternative and politicized media preoccupied with reflecting his own ideals and philosophical principles. Cortéz' response to mainstream news was to analyze it critically according to his vision and perspective of the contemporary world. An experienced individual, Cortéz developed clear and unbreakable convictions. This is reflected through his work and actions, such as the frequent donations of his works, time and labor for the humanist, social or political causes he considered important.

The Printmaker and His Influences

When interviewing Cortéz about what motivated him to create art and when he began to think about art, he responded:

> I always did some kind of drawing as a small kid. I grew up during the big depression and my parents always saw that I had drawing materials available to use. My father would go without cigarettes to make sure I had materials. It was something where I had developed an aptitude and a liking for making pictures. My parents weren't like others who would say: OK that is very nice, when are you going to do something useful? So, through grammar school I drew, illustrated lessons and made poster projects. In high school I attended art classes where I learned linoleum relief graphics (circa 1939-40). The class would put out a booklet from the students every year.
>
> Later when I lived by myself and worked in construction, I decided to take some unaccredited evening art classes as a means of self discipline. While I was making good money, as a young person I didn't want to just burn a hole in my pocket and spend it on a lot of frivolities. Through these classes I learned sculpture, oil painting and figure drawing. Years later when I started to do cartoons for the IWW paper they could no longer afford to make plates from drawings. I saw there was an old timer from California who did linoleum blocks like this (pointing to his own) and I thought I could do the same thing.

The linoleum blocks came already mounted on wood and were the right height for use in a type-high press. Linoleum was a resilient and durable material which allowed one to print as many as 30,000 prints and more. When the reproduction process changed again and offset printing was adopted, Cortéz returned to drawing illustrations for union posters.

While Cortéz always knew he was inspired by and enjoyed making art, it was not until he retired that he was able to completely devote himself to his artistic production. "After having worked for forty years as a construction worker, vendor of records, book seller, factory stiff and janitor, I no longer have to punch a timecard, and I find myself involved in the most productive phase of my life."

He credited his German mother for having helped him develop his "raza" consciousness:

> Even though I resembled my German mother more than my Mexican father, being the only Mexican in a school full of whites made me mighty soon realize who I was. But it was my German mother who started my Mexican consciousness. She said, "Son, don't let the children at school call you a foreigner. Through your father you are Indian and that makes you more American than any of them.[7]

As a child, while supported by his parents, he showed a strong interest in printmaking, drawing and painting to which he was exposed during his high school years and the night classes he took for a couple of years. It was precisely there that his teachers were the first to tell him two things. On one hand, his early works shared some characteristics and similarities with the work of José Clemente Orozco (1883-1949). Orozco was just one of the three great Mexican muralists whose works Cortéz had never seen. He then began researching and learning about them. Soon he learned about the strength in his parents' cultural heritage. He was pleased to realize that Mexican history didn't begin with Hernán Cortes's conquest but, instead, dated back in time for thousands of years. During this true period of research, Cortéz came across José Guadalupe Posada and the many other artists who utilized the calavera or skeleton image. However, he would not learn the Day of the Dead tradition, its meaning and use of calaveras and the varied richness of this tradition until later.

7 Cortéz quoted in "Art People: Carlos Cortéz, Mexican German Expressionist," by Aaron Cohen in *Chicago Reader*, July 23, 1993.

On the other hand, an art teacher in one of his night art classes identified elements that Cortéz' work shared with the German Expressionist Käthe Kollwitz (1867-1945). Cortéz then went to do research again, and to his surprise he saw how, in addition to Kollwitz, his work shared elements with Edward Munch. In 1971, Cortéz traveled with Marianna to Oslo, Norway to visit the Munch Museum. As they approached the museum, Marianna commented on the fact that he was shaking. He agreed with her exclaiming, "This is a pilgrimage for me." Such is the sense of affinity that one artist can experience with another and how deep the feelings can be from one artist to another.

Cortéz' encounter with Mexican printmaker and illustrator José Guadalupe Posada led him to the graphic production of TGP previously described. The artistic contributions and the art works left by all these artists continued to have an influence on Cortéz' works. He had the opportunity to travel, meet artists, and see their original works in the United States, Germany and México. However, Chicago had its own contemporary Posada in Cortéz who, as Posada did decades earlier, reflected much of the life of a people, not only of Mexican immigrants but of workers in general.

Posada is considered the father of Mexican modern art; he was the first artist to create an original and new direction, a sort of new strain that emerged from the predominant European colonial art canon, which subsequently crystallized and formed the foundation for Mexican Modern Art. A prolific artist, Posada produced an estimated 20,000 images including lithographs, lead engravings and especially relief prints or zincographs. Posada can be easily identified by his playful and at times satirical calaveras that are now known in much of the world. He was one of the first Mexican artists to pictorially depict poor Mexican workers and peasants and to show how in death, the Mexican elites (religious leaders, politicians and even artists) shared the same fate as everyone else. So, in "La Catrina," Posada portrays death as the great equalizer.

"Portrait of José Guadalupe Posada and His Catrina" (2002)
From: The Permanent Collection of the National Museum of Mexican Art

Posada's classic image has penetrated Mexican popular and fine art and has influenced fine artists from many countries. This image has become one of the most representative images of Mexican identity. This is without a doubt one of the most famous calaveras which is reborn year after year in the minds of every generation of artisans.

It is within this context and within this artistic frame and tradition that Cortéz places himself. As one of the artists influenced by Posada, Cortéz takes his turn in continuing the graphic tradition in the United States and, in this way, pays homage to this illustrious artist. One of Cortéz' sharpest works is precisely a 1981 print dedicated to the memory of Posada titled *Homage to Posada*.

With his singular style, Cortéz brought Posada back to life in a certain and expressive portrait shown carving several calaveras. Unlike his own death, lonely and abandoned, Posada is depicted with his loyal companion, his famous creation, "La Catrina." The skeleton projects a sense of tranquility and affectionately rests her arm over Posada's shoulder. Cortéz' intention seems to have been to bring them together as a couple, as impossible as this may seem. However, in Cortéz' graphic virtual world this becomes real. They are shown as a congenial couple, relating to one another, with support and understanding. The skeleton reflects support and understanding while the image of Posada reflects sincerity, dedication and certainty.

Cortéz as Artist-Communicator

Cortéz' philosophy of life, his way of facing problems quietly and with knowledge, won him the respect and a special place in the hearts of all who knew him. Such people included local artists, those from other states where he has traveled, as well as those of the general public who had the fortune of meeting him and enjoying his art. Before anything else, philosophically he was an artist who produced art for the purpose of communicating. He considered himself a communicator who happened to utilize the artistic media to share his ideas on a number of issues. What he considered relevant were not numbered and signed edition of prints, rather, it was the content, the idea, and the art's message.

I remember once while at an opening reception in Chicago's Peace Museum for the show *Committed To Print*, Cortéz' wife Marianna came to me looking for my support and approval, as she asked me, right in front of Cortéz, "Don't you think Carlos needs to pay more attention to the printing process? Look at his works in the show; his pieces are the only ones not printed cleanly and clearly. Wouldn't his work look better if it were well printed? I have always told him he must improve on this, but he never listens to me."

While agreeing with her, I explained that it would be to his benefit to improve the printing quality, but another issue needed to be considered. Because Cortéz had pulled so many prints in a particular way, most people were familiar with his approach. His collectors knew, appreciated, and collected his works in that shape; with uneven inking, not perfect, and with irregularities on texture and paper. It has become part of his work's identity; it is now a characteristic the public has not only come to know, but to expect. This may be positive or negative, since many of his works are printed on the various papers he found, and this adds a special touch to each work. Some papers were metallic, and others had printed patterns. Other works were printed while he participated in producing portfolios and other collective projects. In such cases, his works have a different appearance.

The Iconography

José Guadalupe Posada, like Cortéz, was able to communicate to the public a whole story making use of simplified and graphically strong images. This quality proved to be valuable and effective during Posada's time, at the end of the 19th century and beginning of the twentieth century in Mexico. From the 1950s on, it proved equally effective for Cortéz. From his early works concerning farm workers, Day of the Dead and commemorative posters to his homage to heroes in the 1980s and 90s, Cortéz' works are evidence of the graphic power of communication that this artist developed.

Cortéz assimilated Posada's tendencies, and in his works this quality transcends beyond location and time. He applied them to his contemporary world utilizing the double property, just as Posada did, of images and text to take a snapshot of accounts taken place during his time. Most often, Cortéz' graphic quality predominates over the complementary texts. The graphic tradition for social and political concerns that Posada passed down to the Taller de Gráfica Popular members, the Chicano Movement artists and Cortéz were not unique. Other artists in other times and places have equally been enraged by injustices committed at the hands of those who have abused their power. Francisco Goya y Lucientes dedicated a series of works called *Desastres de la Guerra*, or *The Disasters of War*.

In the case of Posada, his was a response to the extreme conditions created by the thirty-year regime of Dictator Porfirio Díaz. Diaz's centralized cultural and industrial modernization projects increased the extreme poles of the rich elites and the poor masses. This situation prompted the rural working class, in the north and the south, to rebel against the regime in what became known as the Mexican Revolution of 1910. In the 1960s and 70s, the Chicano Movement artists included graphic responses to the problems faced by rural agricultural workers throughout the United States—above all, the low wages and poor labor conditions of farmworkers. These issues, along with the Chicano civil rights and student movements, became a unifying cause for the resistance to injustice and the affirmation of a positive Chicano cultural identity.[8] This identity as expressed through graphic art was defined, in the early stages, by artists who, like Cortéz, were influenced by Posada and the TGP among others.

Cortéz didn't grow up in a Mexican cultural environment, as was the case with many artists involved with the Chicano Movement or, locally, with Chicago's Mexicano-Chicano political resistance. Initially, he did not identify himself as a Mexican artist or Chicano for that matter. It was not until he received some recognition as a Chicano artist that he began associating and identifying more directly with the Mexican culture. Thus, Cortéz decided to change his birth name Carl for Carlos and later adopted the indigenous name Koyokuikatl. In the mid-seventies in Chicago, he began to participate in the Chicano

8 La Causa, *Chicano Art: Resistance And Affirmation* (The Wight Art Gallery, University of California, Los Angeles, 1991), 234. Exhibition catalogue.

Movement through MARCH. He along with Mario Castillo, José Gamaliel González, Sal Vega, José Nario, Rey Vásquez, Victor Sorell, María Enríquez de Allen, Harold Allen, Ray Patlán, Marguerite Ortega, Efrain Martínez and others were among the initial active members. He felt this organization received him with open arms, even though, as he stated, "he was only half raza" alluding to the fact that only half of his heritage is Mexican. Over several decades, the images Cortéz created became icons of the Chicano-Mexicano community.

Final Considerations

Up until the death of his wife Marianna, Cortéz seemed quite happy and satisfied with life. He was especially proud to have gotten recognition for his artistic contributions while he was still alive, in particular, the recognition by other artists, the "Wobblies," and the people in places where he has done artistic, cultural, solidarity and labor work. By the end of the twentieth century, two collections in the US included all or most of his works: the Mexican Fine Arts Center Museum and the Center for the Study of Political Graphics in California. His purpose in donating these collections had been to share his work with other generations of working people as well as those interested in his work and ideas. The grateful acceptance of these collections fed his ego, a fact he mentioned to his friends on more than one occasion. One of Cortéz' goals was to make sure his works would always be accessible for purchase. He hoped that, if in any given moment, the value of his prints went high, because of market speculators, someone would print large numbers again from his original plates. This would surely bring prices down and maintain accessibility of his work to common people. The following verse by Cortéz synthesizes, in a clear way, his convictions and reveals his persona as a human being thinker and writer:

Untitled

An idea does not become
trapped in one person.
If the person has an idea
and does not give it freedom
it will escape to someone who will.

You see, ideas are very promiscuous
but that does not matter.
Ideas are destined
to outlive their liberators.
It is good

Bibliography of Poetry

All items referring to Cortéz' poetic work have been listed as fully as possible. The list combines Cortéz' own literary history written in 1997 with additional citations by the editors and Marc Zimmerman, Professor Emeritus of Latin American and Latino Studies at the University of Illinois, Chicago, who initially compiled a bibliography for *Chicano Writers, Third Series*, Dictionary of Literary Biography, volume 209, 1999.

Cortéz' publication in magazines and newspapers seem to suddenly stop after 1991, and I am speculating that he may have decided to focus his energies on his personal and collaborative visual artwork and offering guided tours to the murals across Chicago. He did continue to make public appearances to read his poetry up until 2003.

—*Carlos Cumpián*

Books

Crystal-Gazing the Amber Fluid & Other Wobbly Poems. Chicago: Charles H. Kerr Publishing Company, 1990. Introduction by Eugene Nelson.

de Kansas a Califas & Back to Chicago: Poems & Art. Chicago: MARCH Abrazo Press, 1992. Foreword by Joel Climenhaga.

Where are the Voices & Other Wobbly Poems. Chicago: Charles H. Kerr Publishing Company, 1997. Introduction by Archie Green.

Tere Romo, ed. *Fanning the Flames.* Chicago: Mexican Fine Arts Center Museum, 2000. Exhibition catalog.

Anthologies and Textbooks

"Outa Work Blues," in *Poets of Today: A New American Anthology*, edited by Walter Lowenfels, 36. New York: International Publishers, 1964.

"Where are the Voices?" and "Digging the Squares at Jack London Square," *Rebel Voices: An IWW Anthology*, edited by Joyce L. Kornbluh, 392, 295. First published 1964 by University of Michigan (Ann Arbor), republished 1988 by Charles H. Kerr Publishing Company (Chicago), and republished 2011 by PM Press (Oakland). Page references are to the original edition.

"Tonatlancihuatl," in *Nahualliandoing: poetry in Español, Nahuatl, English*, edited by Cecilio and Mia García-Camarillo, 13. San Antonio: Caracol Press, 1977.

"May Song," in *Arrangement in Literature*, edited by Edmund J. Farrell, Ovida H. Clapp, James L. Pierce, and Raymond J. Rodrigues, 597. Glenview, IL: Scott Foresman, 1979.

"This is the Land," in *The United States in Literature*, edited by James E. Miller, Carlota Cárdenas de Dwyer, Robert Hayden, Russell J. Hagan, and Kerry M. Wood, 574. Glenview, IL: Scott Foresman, 1979.

Journeys: A Reading and Literature Program, New York: Harcourt Brace Jovanovich, 1982.

"Peregrinaje en Hannibal, Missouri" and "Calabria," in *Canto al Pueblo: Antologia Anthology*, edited by Justo S. Alarcón, Juan Pérez Aldape, and Lupe Cárdenas, 48. Mesa: Arizona Canto al Pueblo, 1980.

"Prelude to the Moment of Truth," "Empty House Blues," "Quo Vadisimus," and "Yosemite," in *Emergency Tacos: Seven Poets con Picante*, edited by Carlos Cumpián, 16-19. Chicago: MARCH Abrazo Press, 1989.

"Las Calándrias," in *Red Dirt: Crosscultural Poetry*, edited by Lorna Dee Cervantes and Jay Griswold, 37. Boulder: Red Dirt Press, 1991.

"Las Calándrias," "Sisters Beneath the Concrete," and "Tenochtitlan," in *Shards of Light/Astillas de Luz*, edited by Olivia Maciel, 19-25. Chicago: Tia Chucha Press, 1998.

"Requiem for 'Two Dago Reds'" and "Three Spirits: Frank Little, Wesley Everest, and Joe Hill," in *Working Words: Punching the Clock and Kicking Out the Jams*, edited by M.L. Liebler. Minneapolis, Coffee House Press, 2010. Foreword by Ben Hamper.

Journals and Magazines

"My poetry first appeared in the *Industrial Worker* in the late 1950s, and my poems and other writings, as well as graphic art, have appeared in that journal through the present."

Iskra #791 (1960). Poems translated into Russian.

Beatitude/east #17 (1961). New York, NY.

"The Smith" 7 (1966). New York, NY.

Souvenir booklet of Joe Hill Museum. Gävle, Sweden, 1973. Poems translated into Swedish.

Quixote, vol. LV, no. 1 (1969-1979). Chicago.

"Macuilhaicuh." *Revista Chicano-Riqueña* 4, no. 3 (Summer 1976): 3. Five haiku in Spanish.

"Where are the Voices?" *Grito del Sol: A Chicano Quarterly* 3, book 2 or 3 (1978). Canto Al Pueblo Issue devoted to the poets that performed at the first Canto Al Pueblo, Milwaukee, WI in May 1977. His name was misspelled Cortes.

Nit & Wit: A Literary Arts Journal (1981). Chicago. Haiku in Spanish.

"Houn' Dog." *ECOS: A Latino Journal of People's Culture & Literature* 2, no. 1 (1982): 17. University of Illinois, Chicago.

"Chickens on the Top" and "Enganadora." *ECOS: A Latino Journal of People's Culture & Literature* 3 (1985): 28-29.

Notebook: A Little Magazine #2 (1988). California.

Pig Iron: Labor & the Post-Industrial Age #16 (1991). Youngstown, OH.

The Pittsburgh Quarterly 1, no 2 (1991).

"How La Guitarra Was Born." *Rattle: Poetry for the 21st Century* no. 12 (Winter 1999): 100. This issue "A Tribute to Latino & Chicano Poets" celebrated the work of twenty-three poets including Cortéz Koyokuikatl.

Exhibition History

Solo Exhibiciones

Galería Julio Ruelas, Zacatecas, *Gráfica Chicana de Carlos Cortéz*, January 1988.

Mexican Fine Arts Center Museum, Chicago, *The Graphic Works of Carlos Cortéz*, December 1988-January 1989.

Chicano Humanities and Arts Council (CHAC), Denver, *Las Obras de Carlos Cortéz*, September 1989.

Teikyo-Westman University, Le Mars, Iowa, February 1993.

Mexican Fine Arts Center Museum, Chicago, *Fanning the Flames*, July-August 1997 (traveled on tour).

Carlos Cortéz Archive. Permanent Collection. National Museum of Mexican Art, Chicago.

Group Exhibitions

Chicago State University Gallery, *Hispanic-American Art in Chicago*, June-July 1980.

Galería de la Raza, San Francisco, *El Día de los Muertos*, November 1982.

Mexican Fine Arts Center Museum, *Art of the Other Mexico*, June 1983 (traveled on tour).

Centro de Económicos y Sociales del Tercer Mundo, Mexico City, *A través de la frontera*, August-September 1983.

Statliche Kunsthalle, Berlin, *Das Andere Amerika*, August-September 1983 (travelled on tour throughout Europe).

Galería Ink Works, Chicago, *Nuestro Pasado, Nuestro Presente*, November 1985.

Galería de la Ciudad de México, *Artistas Latinoamericanos en Chicago*, 1986.

Mexican Fine Arts Center Museum, Chicago, *The Barrio Murals*, July-September 1987.

Museum of Modern Art, New York, NY, *Committed to Print*, January-April 1988.

Mexican Fine Arts Center, Chicago, *El Día de los Muertos*, October-December 1988, 1989.

Wight Art Gallery, University of California, Los Angeles, *Chicano Art-Resistance & Affirmation (CARA)* 1965-1985, December 1988-January 1989 (travelled on tour).

Carlos A. Cortéz at the José Guadalupe Posada Aguilar traveling exhibition opening night December 16, 1988 at Chicago's Mexican Fine Arts Center 1852 West 19th Street, Chicago, IL; renamed as the National Museum of Mexican Art. Photo by Carlos Cumpián.

"...Through his words and woodcuts Cortéz is a delightful and important chronicler of labor movements, Chicano history and, of course, la vida. We do well in lending him an ear, an eye, a moment of our busy time. This is how we prepare to be human—by stopping to pay respect, to learn from, make use of the gifts an artist and activist among us has for so long so generously offered. Te saludo, don Carlos"

Ana Castillo,
Author of *Doña Cleanwell Leaves Home: Stories* (2023)

Carlos Cumpián is a Chicagoan originally from Texas. *Human Cicada* (Prickly Pear Publishing, 2022) marks his fifth poetry collection. His earlier works are *Coyote Sun* (MARCH Abrazo Press), *Latino Rainbow* (Children's Press/Scholastic Books), *Armadillo Charm* (Tia Chucha), and *14 Abriles: Poems* (MARCH Abrazo Press, 2010). In 2000, he was recognized with a Gwendolyn Brooks Significant Illinois Poet Award. Cumpián has been included in more than thirty poetry anthologies, including the Norton Anthology *Telling Stories*. He has been active in Chicano Indigenous empowerment since the early 1970s both in electoral politics and in cultural expressions. MARCH Abrazo Press was where he served as the organization's Coordinador General and Editor for their mainly poetry publications and public readings between 1982 to 2012.

He taught English full-time in the Chicago Public Schools system from 1995 to 2016 and poetry at Columbia College Chicago for nine years. He has also offered writing workshops through the Illinois Arts Council Writers-in Residence programs in Cook County. Prior to teaching he worked in Public Relations for Chicago's Public Library and for Chicago's Dept. of Housing. He has belonged to two unions: The Industrial Workers of the World (IWW Chicago chapter) and the Chicago Teacher's Union. He is on the national board of the non-profit educational group MeXicanos 2070, promoting an online series on Chicano studies. Currently he is working on a series of supernatural accounts, such as "A Chicago Premonition" published in *Hombre Lobo #2: True Xicanax Spooky Stories* (Ponte Las Pilas Press, 2020). Cumpián is also writing his "anti-war years" poetic memoir *Accidental Rebel*: 1968-1976.

David Ranney is Professor Emeritus in the College of Urban Planning and Public Affairs at the University of Illinois Chicago. He received his BA degree at Dartmouth College and his PhD at Syracuse University. Professor Ranney has also been a factory worker, a labor and community organizer and an activist academic. He is the author of four books, a play and numerous articles and monographs on issues of employment, labor and community organizing and US trade policy. His recent book, *Living and Dying on the Factory Floor* (PM Press, 2019) is a memoir of his time as a factory worker in Southeast Chicago factories. Some of his recent essays and books may be found at www.david-ranney.com. In addition to his writing, he gives lectures on economic policy and politics and finds time to be an actor and director in a small community theatre. He is married and has a son, daughter-in-law, and two granddaughters. He splits his time between Chicago and Washington Island, Wisconsin.

Made in the USA
Monee, IL
17 July 2023